Prep Handwriting

Susan Young

illustrations by Janice Bowles and Marta Tesoro

My name is

____

Introduction

This workbook introduces the Prep student to the Queensland Beginner's Alphabet. This particular handwriting style uses simple flowing natural hand movements. The movement patterns include gently sloped straight lines, anti-clockwise and clockwise rotations.

Letters in this workbook are grouped according to these movement patterns. The simple sloped downward straight-line movement is introduced first. More complex movements are introduced later in the book, allowing the student to build on their prior knowledge and move from the simple to more complex movements.

BASIC MOVEMENTS COVERED:

Section one Straight line	**Section two** Anti-clockwise	**Section three** Clockwise	Anti-clockwise and clockwise
Downstroke	Movement	'm' pattern	's' pattern
Horizontal	'w' pattern	Loop pattern	
Diagonal upstroke	Loop pattern	'j' pattern and downstroke	
Crisscross			
'z' pattern			

Prep Handwriting Workbook Features

- Instructions and activities are simple and repetitive, allowing the student to concentrate on the writing task.
- Each letter is clearly represented on the top left-hand side of the double page.
- Capital letter and lower-case letter are paired together on the top right-hand side of the page as a tracking activity.
- The starting points are all clearly marked with a red dot followed by directional arrows.
- Trace and track activities explore the shape and formation of each letter, and encourage fluency of movement.
- Illustrations for each activity provide practice of the required movement, are fun and quirky as well as representing the sound each letter makes.
- A blue line at the bottom of the left-hand page provides practice at placing letters onto lines.
- The red and blue line at the bottom of the right-hand page provides practice at placing letters onto lines that will be used in Year 1.
- Cat Illustration - The cat illustration has been used throughout the book as a visual aid that highlights the head, body and/or tail parts of each letter and assists with letter placement. e.g. The letter 'y' is a body and tail letter, the body part sits on the blue line, and the tail hangs below the blue line.
- The basic movement pattern is noted on the bottom of each page as a reference for the teacher.
- Writing of Numerals 1 -10 is included in the last section of the book.

Handy Hint: For good handwriting to occur and be maintained, it is important that the mechanics of handwriting are addressed. These include correct pencil grip, paper position and posture. Spend a few minutes at the beginning of each handwriting lesson, focussing on these vital points.

Please Note: This book is designed as a supplement to the teacher's handwriting programme. It is important that gross motor and fine motor skills are also incorporated into daily lessons, as they are essential for the development of good handwriting skills.

Suggestions for Gross Motor Activities: Balancing, catching, climbing, hopping, jumping, skipping, kicking, rolling, running, throwing and walking help to improve coordination and strength.

Suggestions for Fine Motor Activities: Colouring in, construction, craft, cutting, dot-to-dot, dough/plasticine modelling, drawing, finger plays, hammering, jigsaws, keyboarding, painting, painting with ear buds, pasting, sewing, sorting, threading and weaving.

I hope you and your students enjoy using this book.

Happy handwriting,

Susan Young

Follow the path. Start at the red dot.

Left to right movement - Tracking

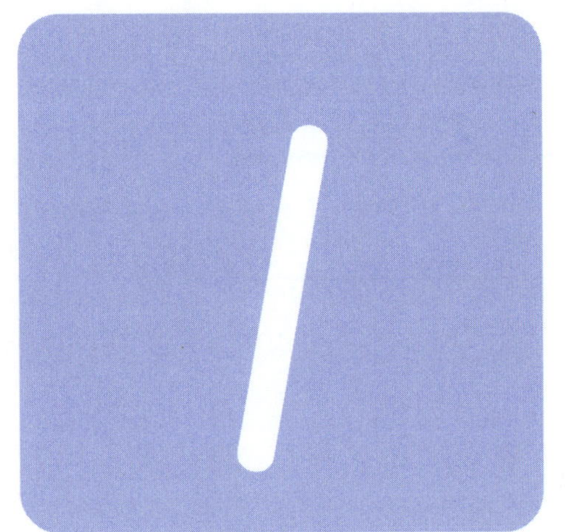

Track. Start at the red dot.

ladders

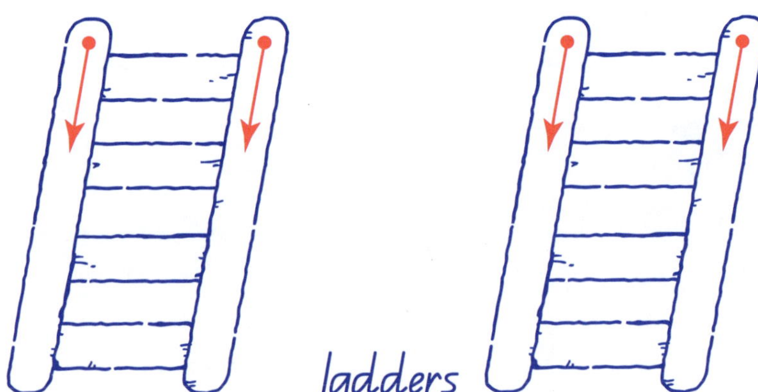

Trace. Start at the red dot.

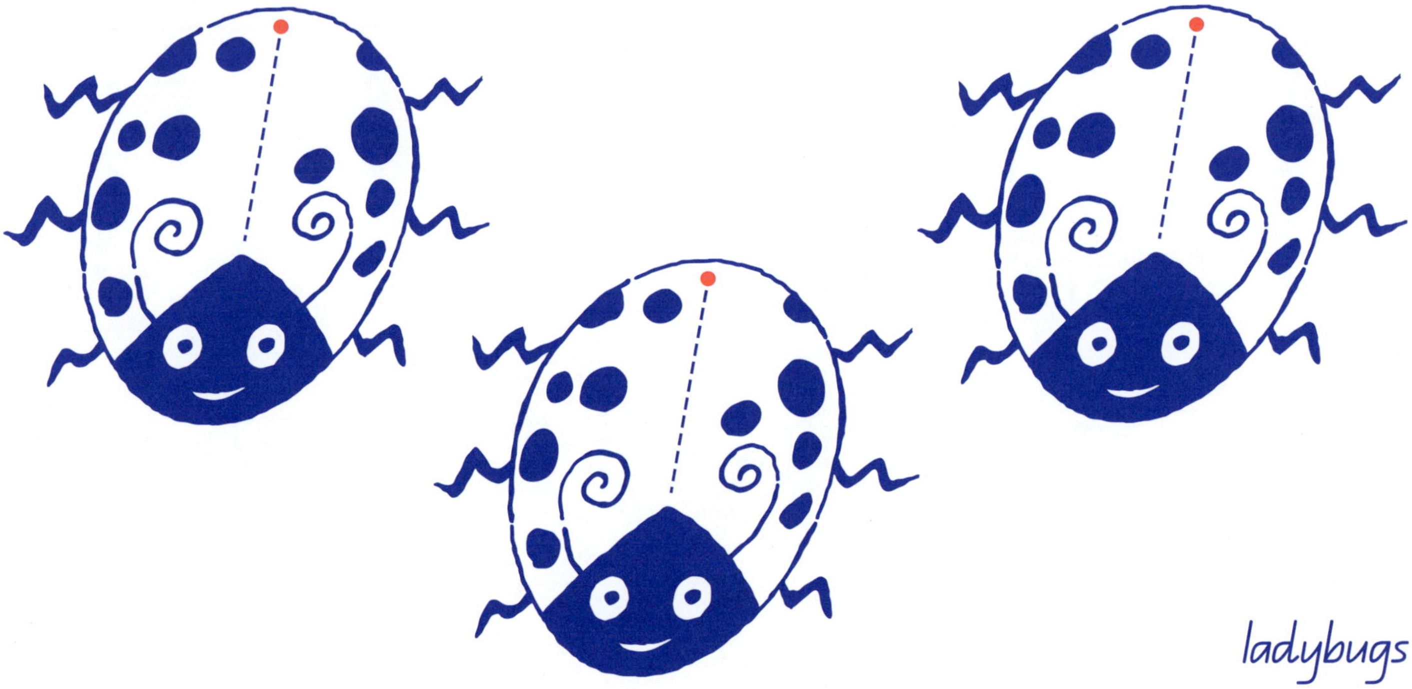

ladybugs

Track.

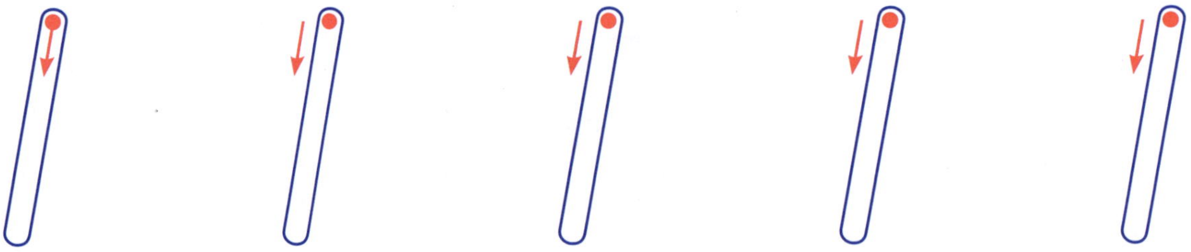

Trace.

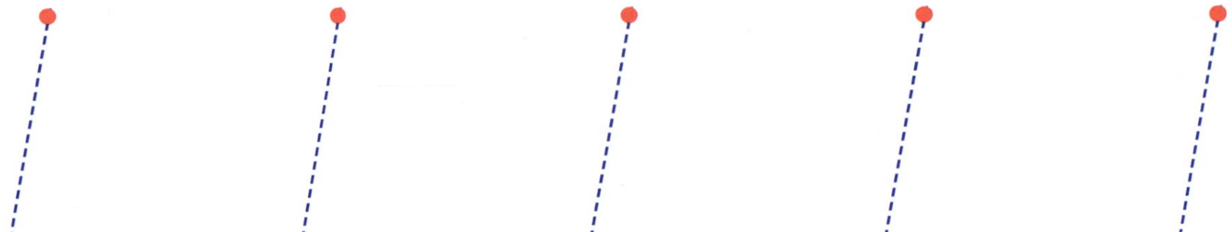

Straight line movement

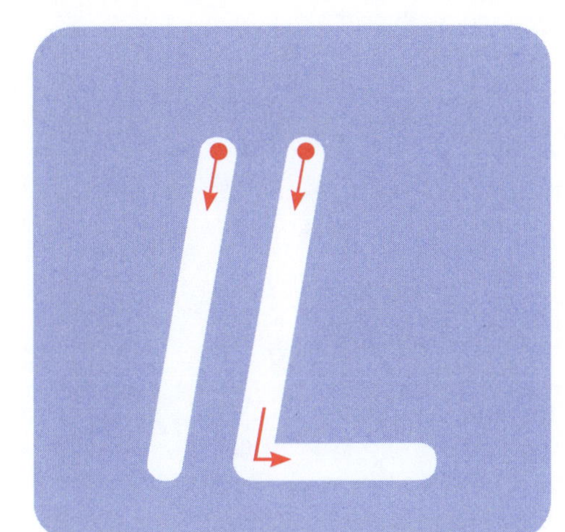

Trace. Start at the red dot.

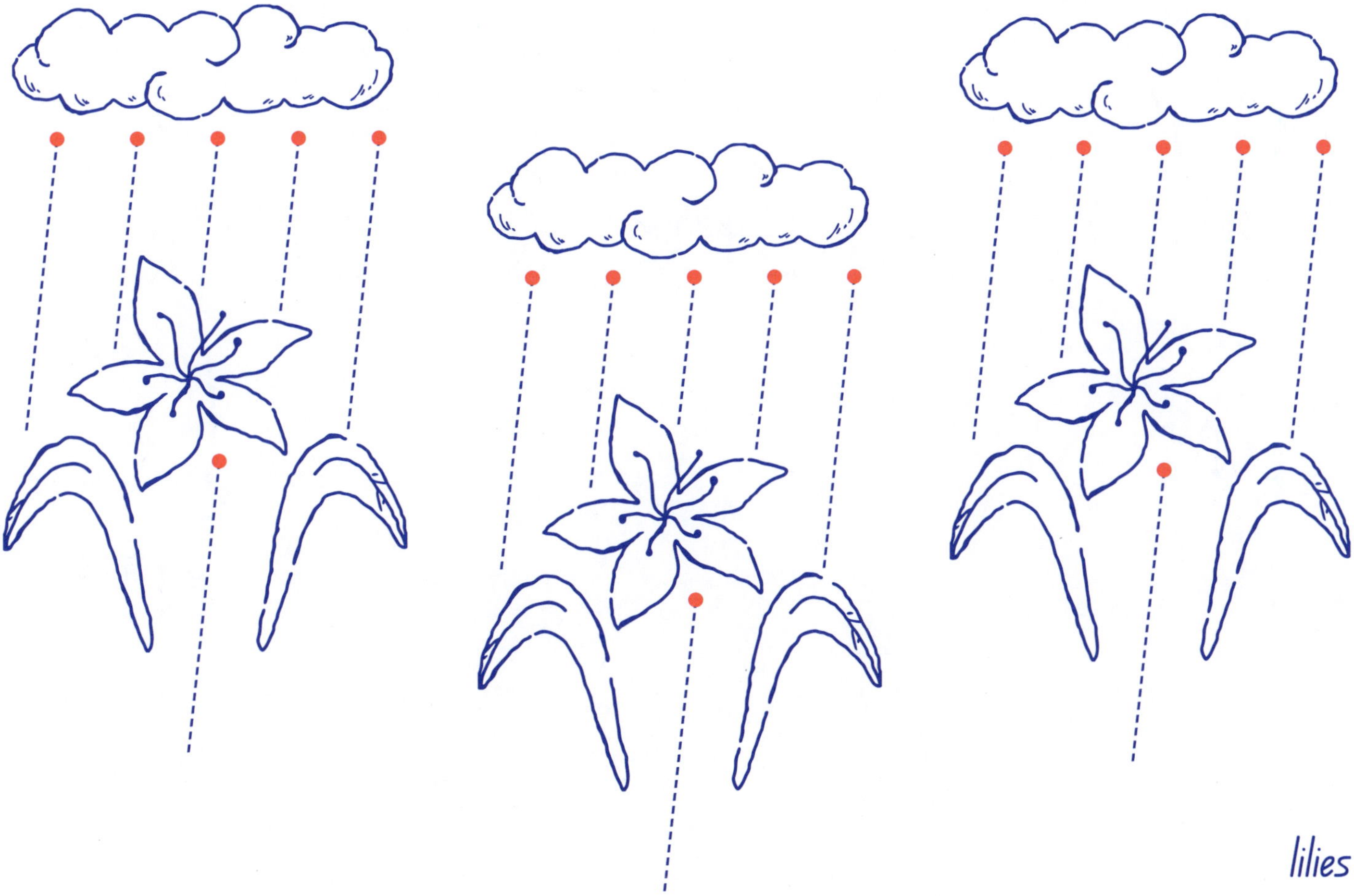

lilies

Trace.

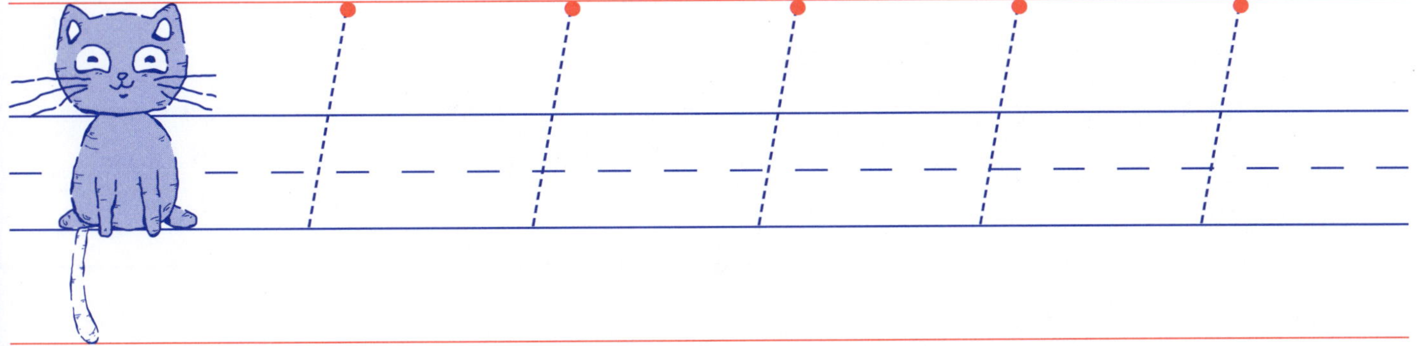

Trace. Start at the red dot.

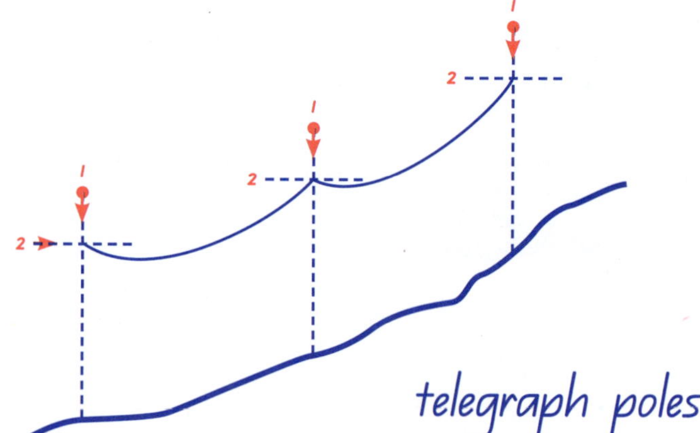

telegraph poles

Trace. Start at the red dot.

t-shirts

Track.

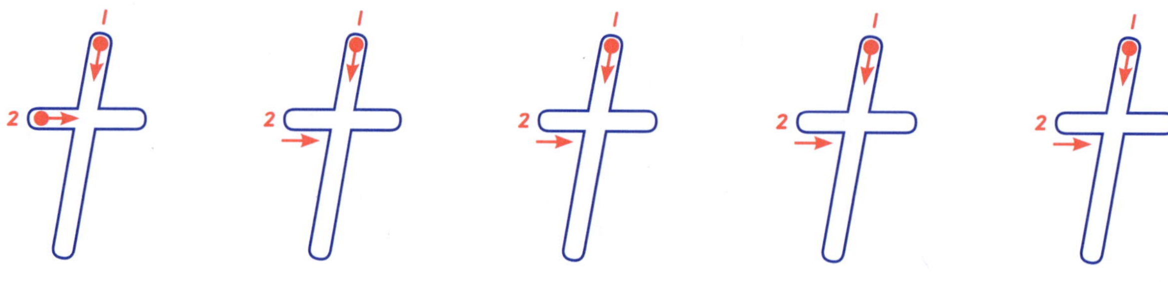

Trace.

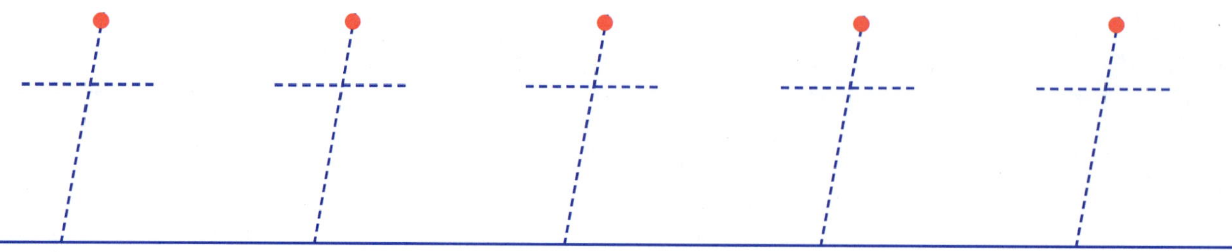

Straight line movement

a head and body letter

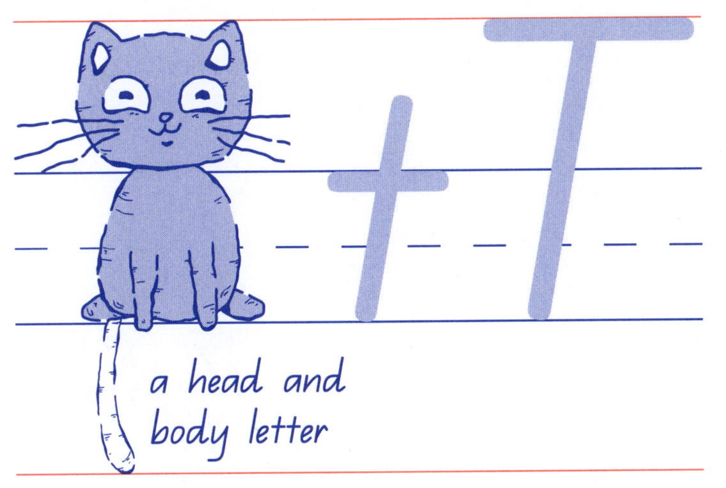

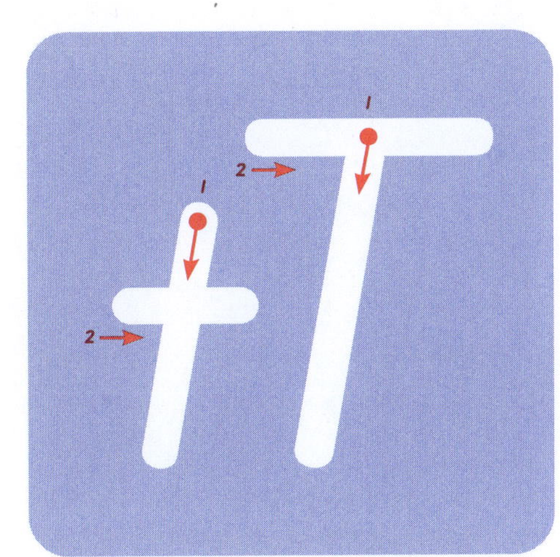

Trace. Start at the red dot.

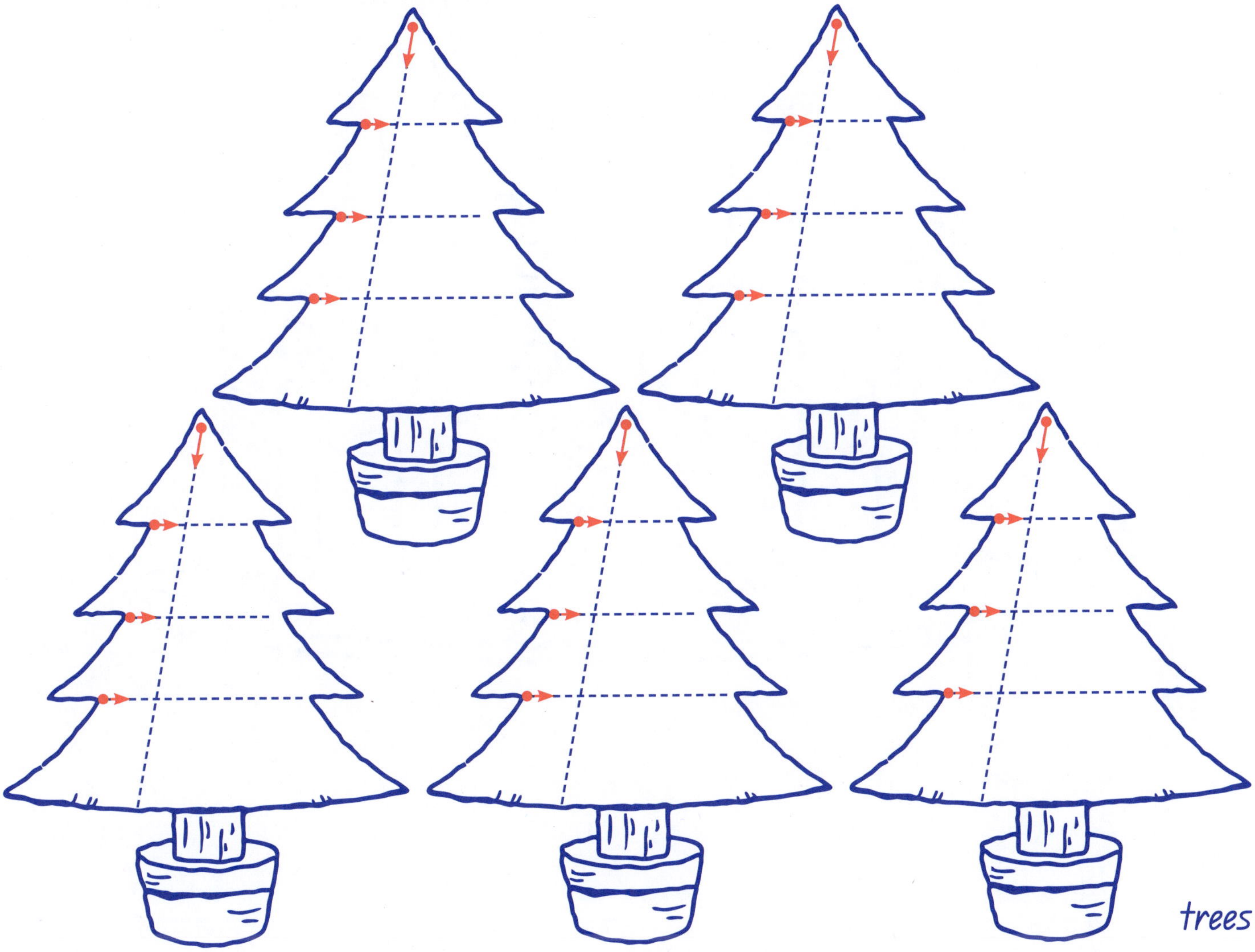

trees

Trace.

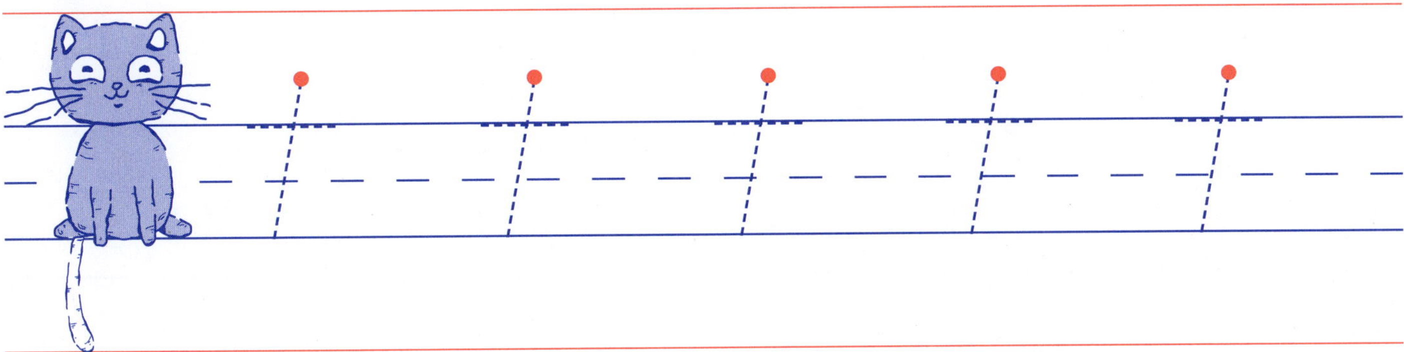

Track. Start at the red dot.

ice-creams

Track. Start at the red dot.

icing

Track.

Trace.

Straight line movement

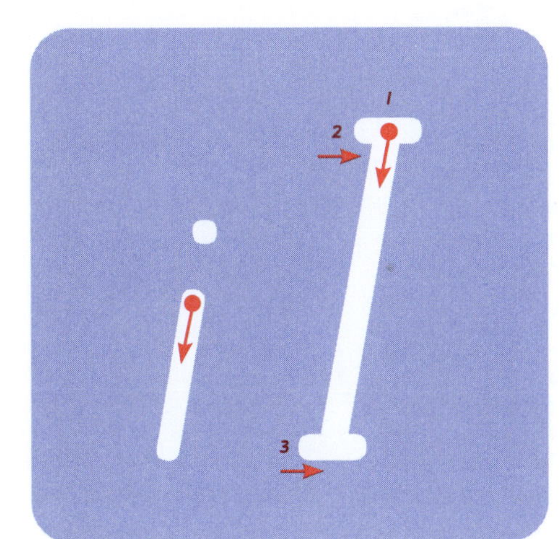

Track. Start at the red dot.

ice-skaters

Trace.

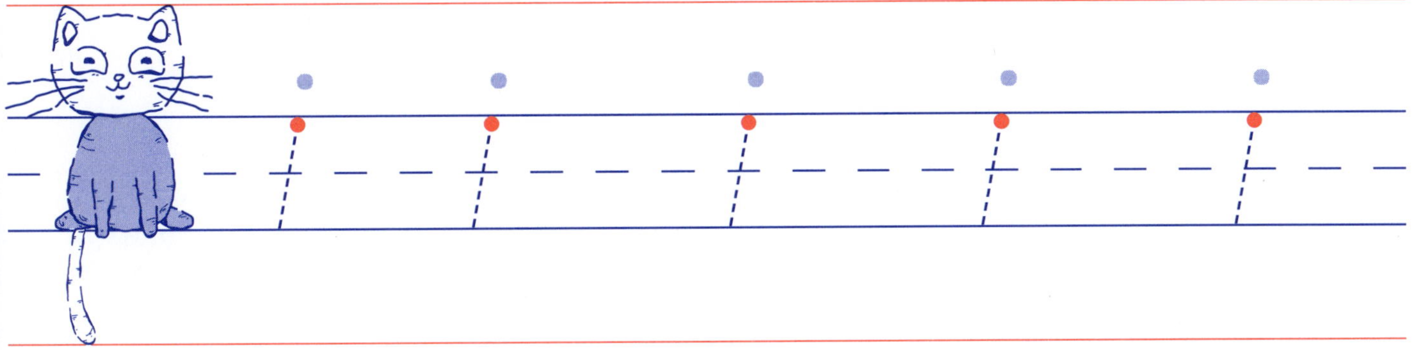

Track. Start at the red dot.

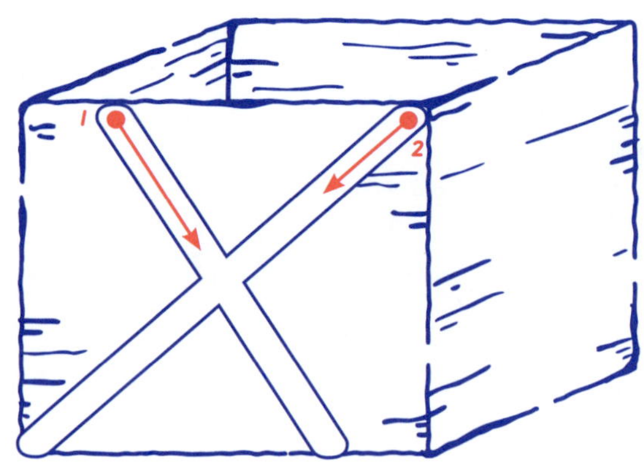

box

Track. Start at the red dot.

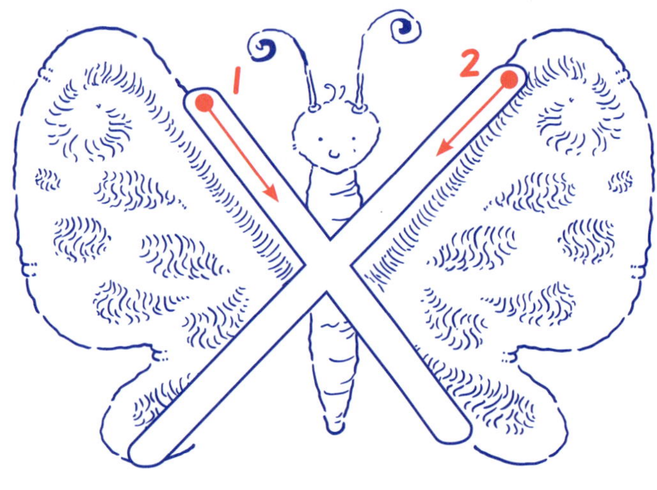

'Xerces Blue' butterflies

Track.

Trace.

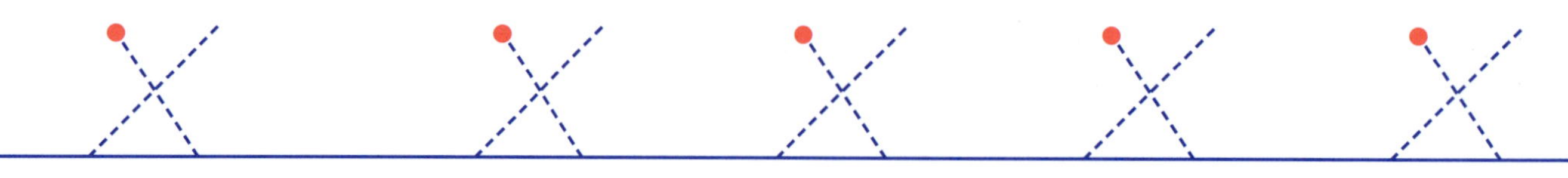

Straight line movement

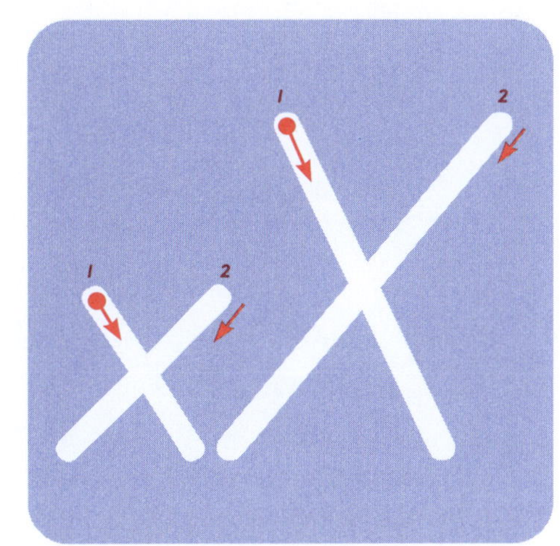

Trace. Start at the red dot.

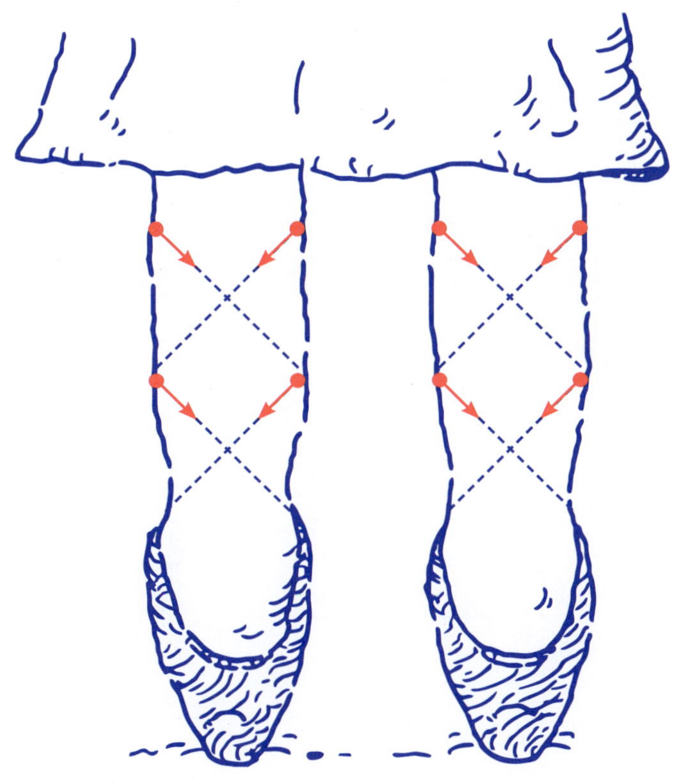

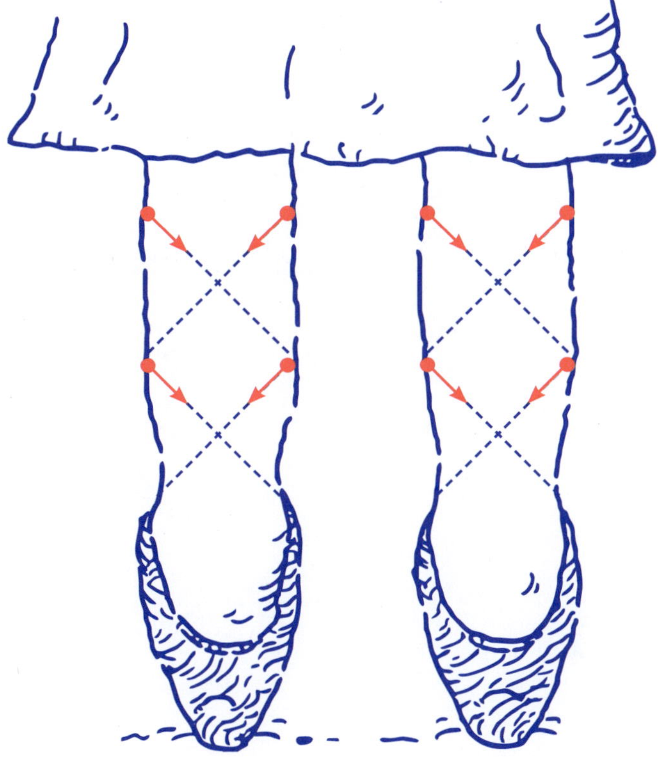

Trace.

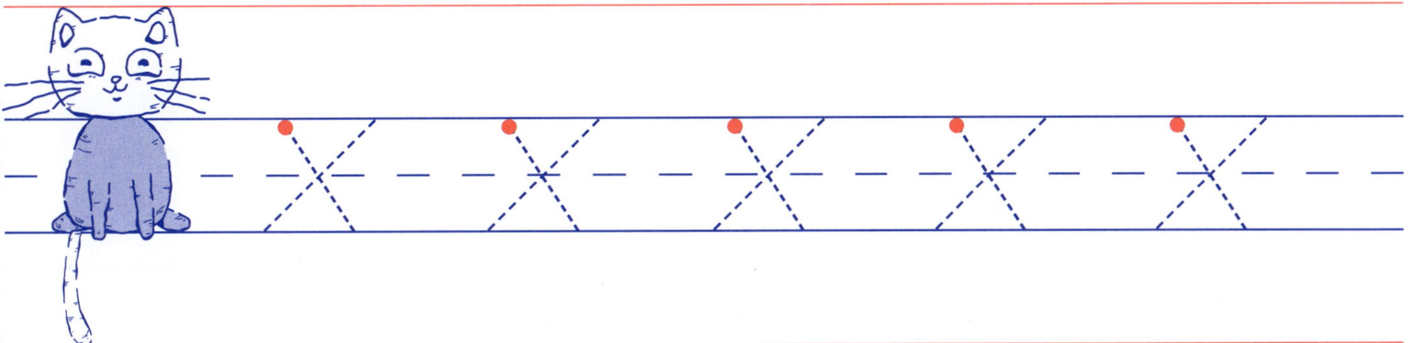

Track. Start at the red dot.

zap

Track. Start at the red dot.

Track.

Trace.

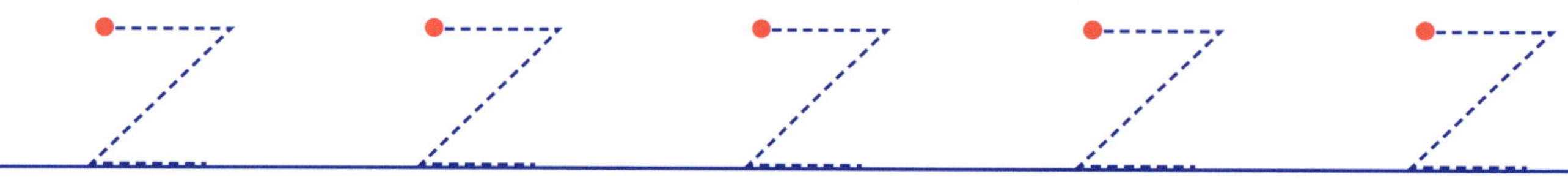

Straight line movement

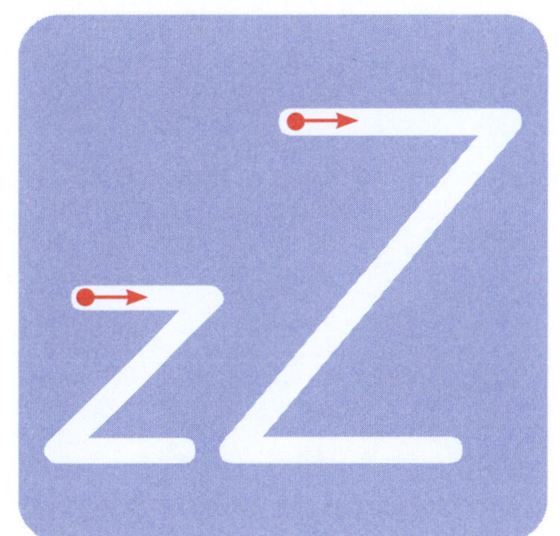

Track. Start at the red dot.

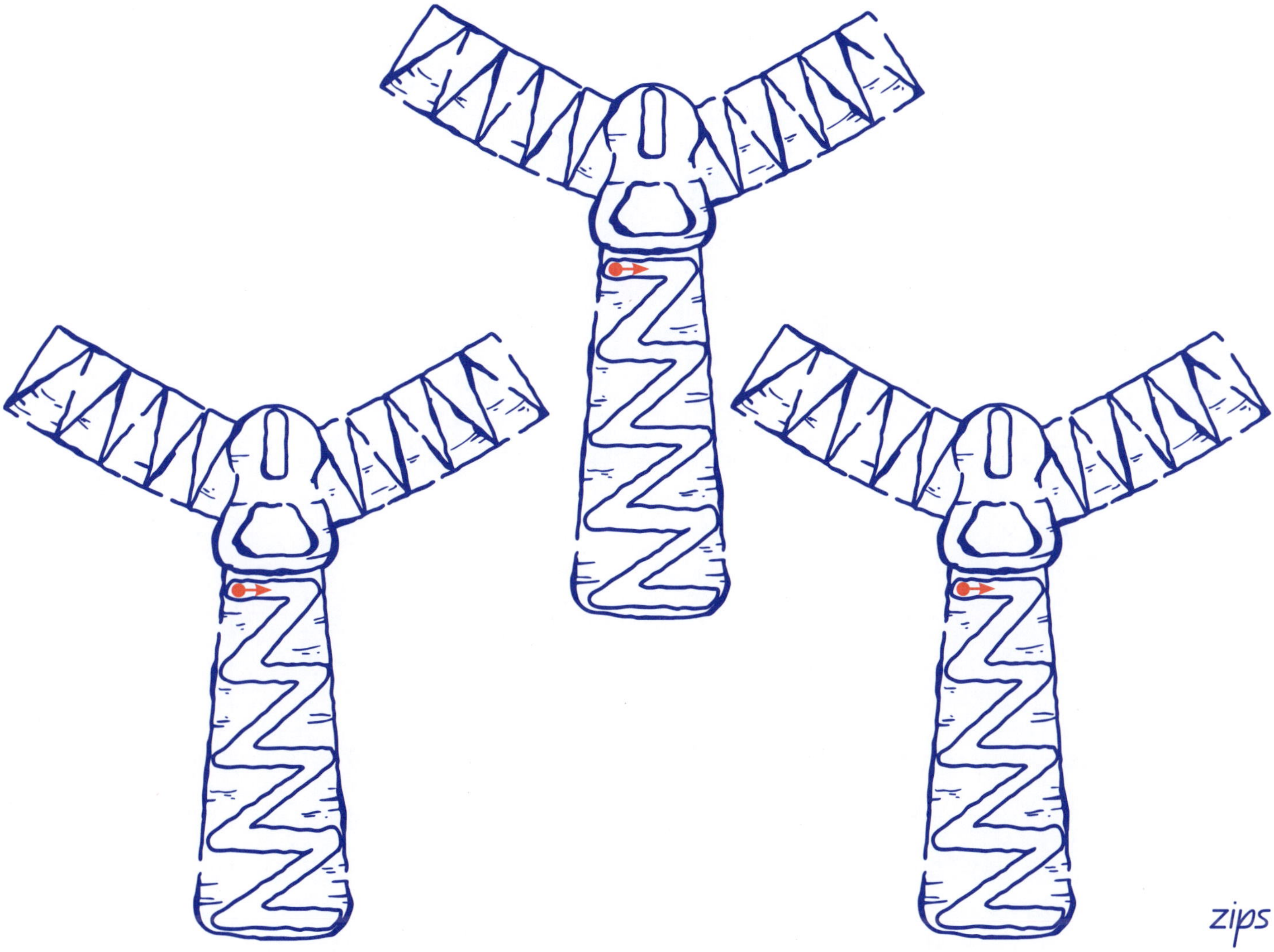

zips

Trace.

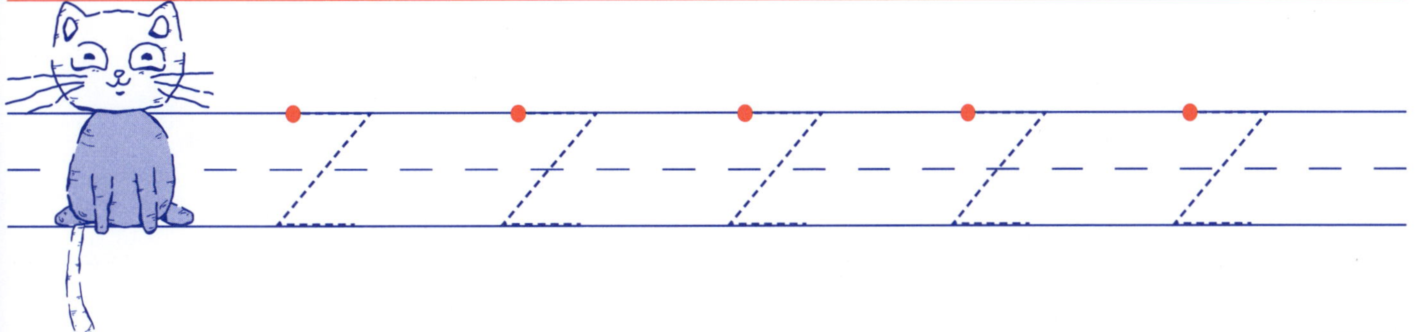

Trace. Start at the red dot.

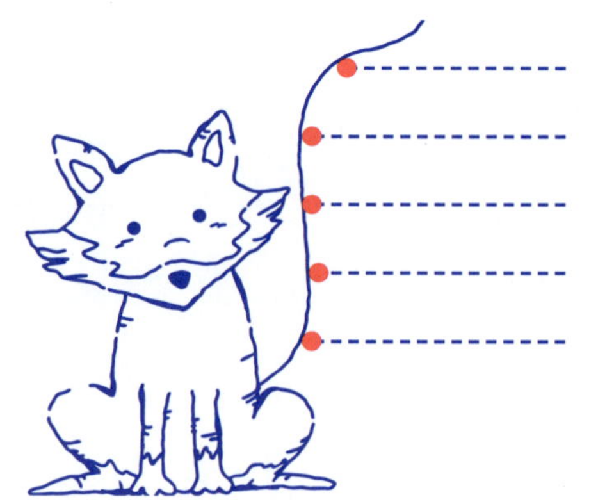

fox

Trace.

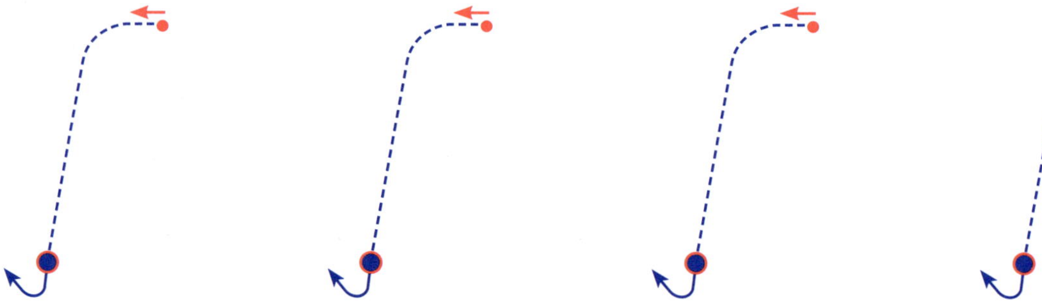

Track.

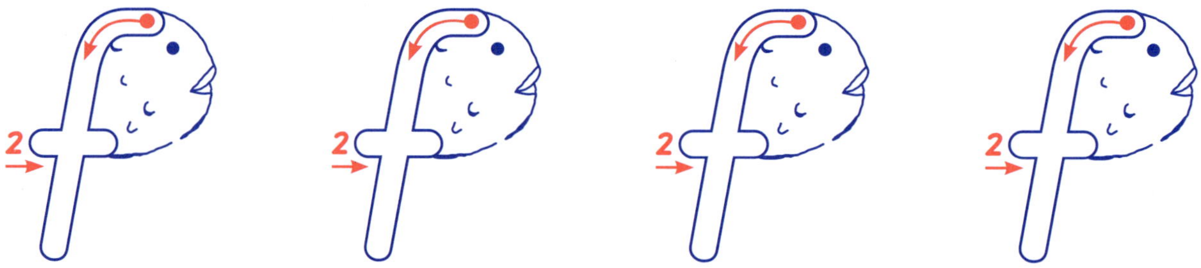

2

fish

Track.

1

2

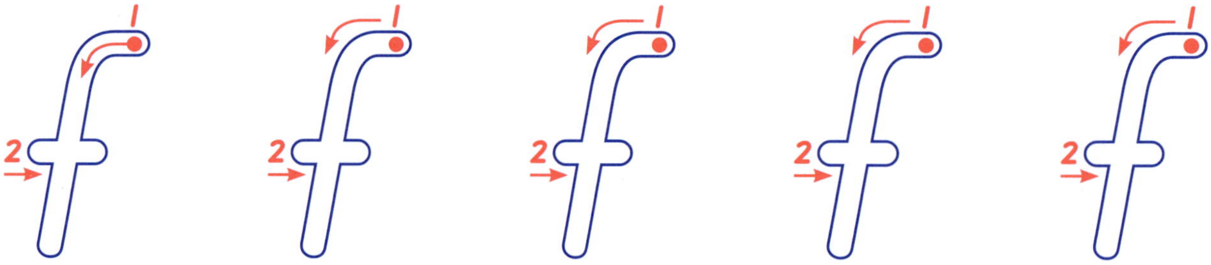

Trace.

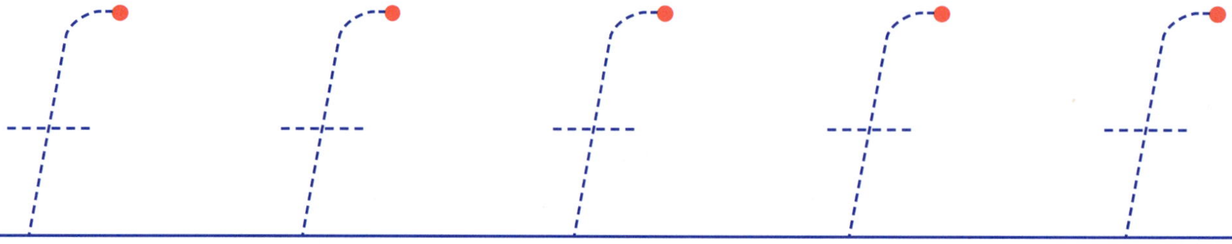

Straight line movement

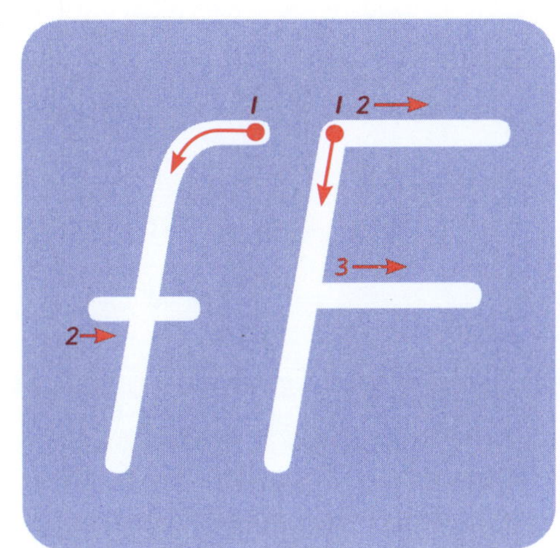

Trace. Start at the red dot.

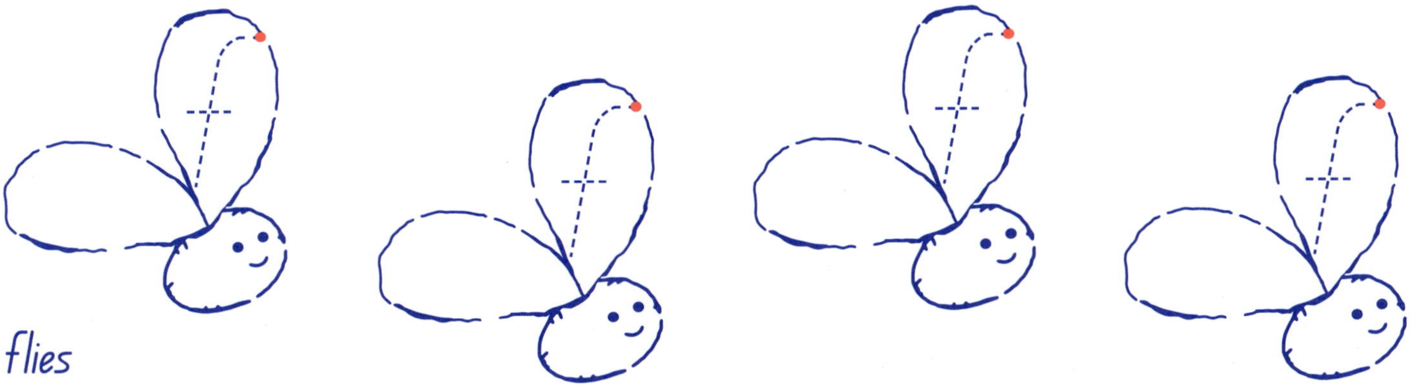

flies

frogs

Trace.

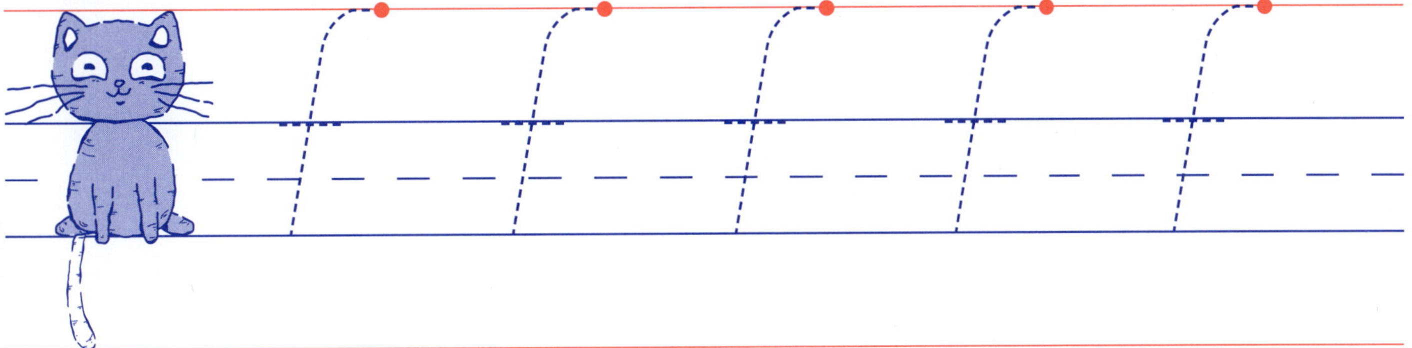

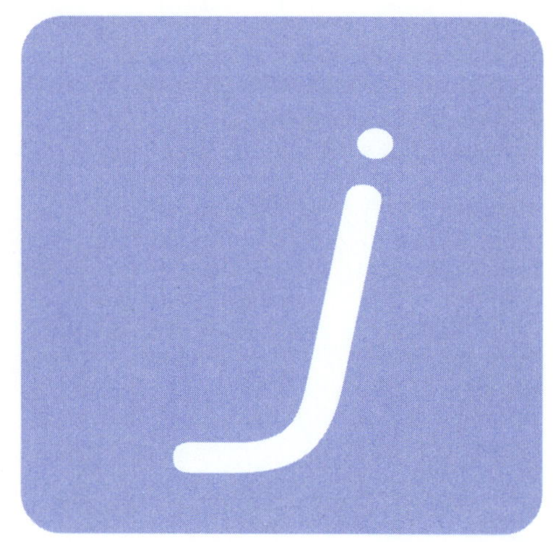

Track. Start at the red dot.

Trace. Start at the red dot.

Jam

Jam

Jam

Jam

Track.

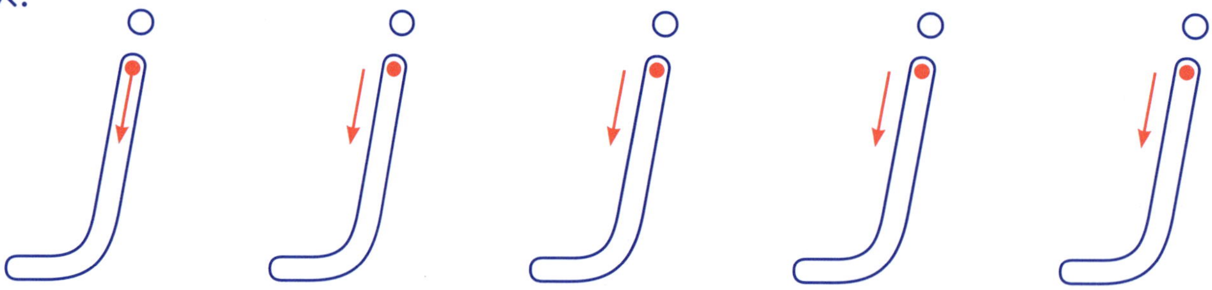

Trace.

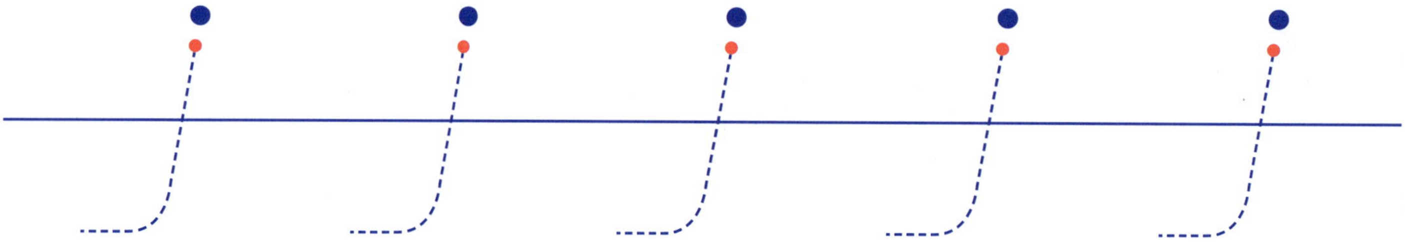

Straight line movement

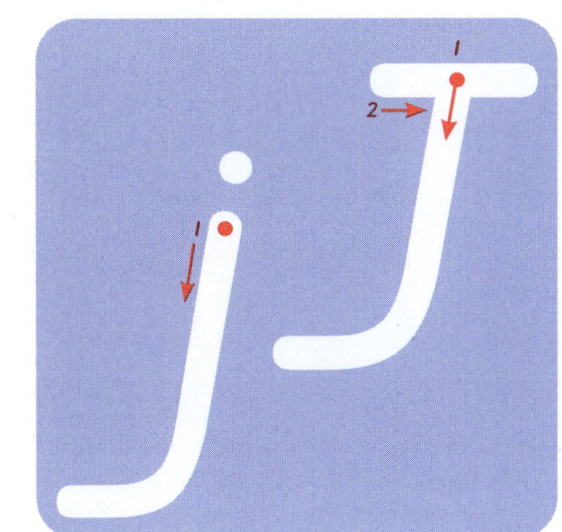

Track. Start at the red dot.

jungle

Trace.

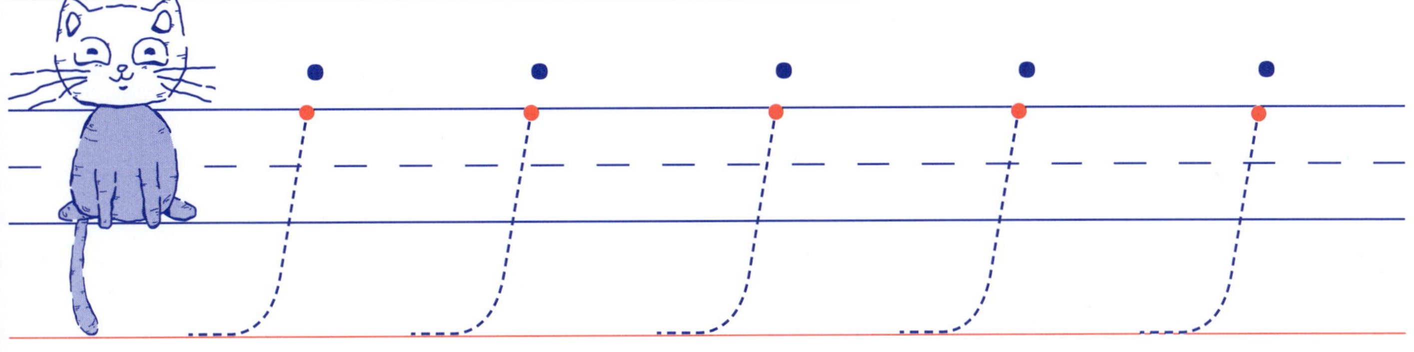

Trace. Start at the red dot.

mountains

Track. Start at the red dot.

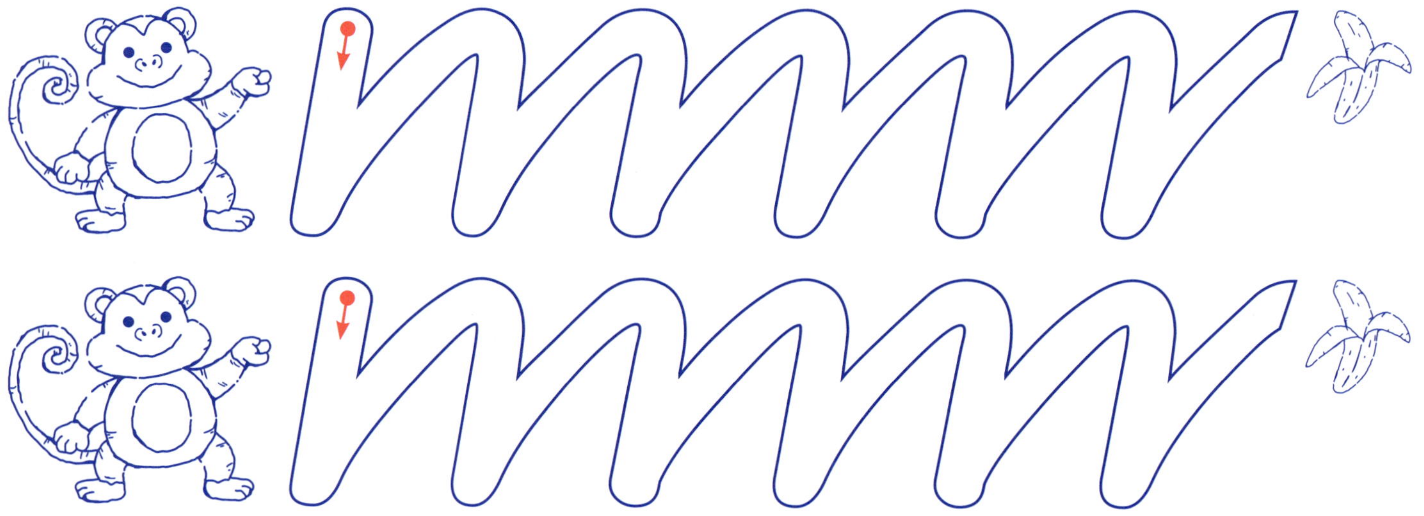

Track.

Trace.

Clockwise movement

Track. Start at the red dot.

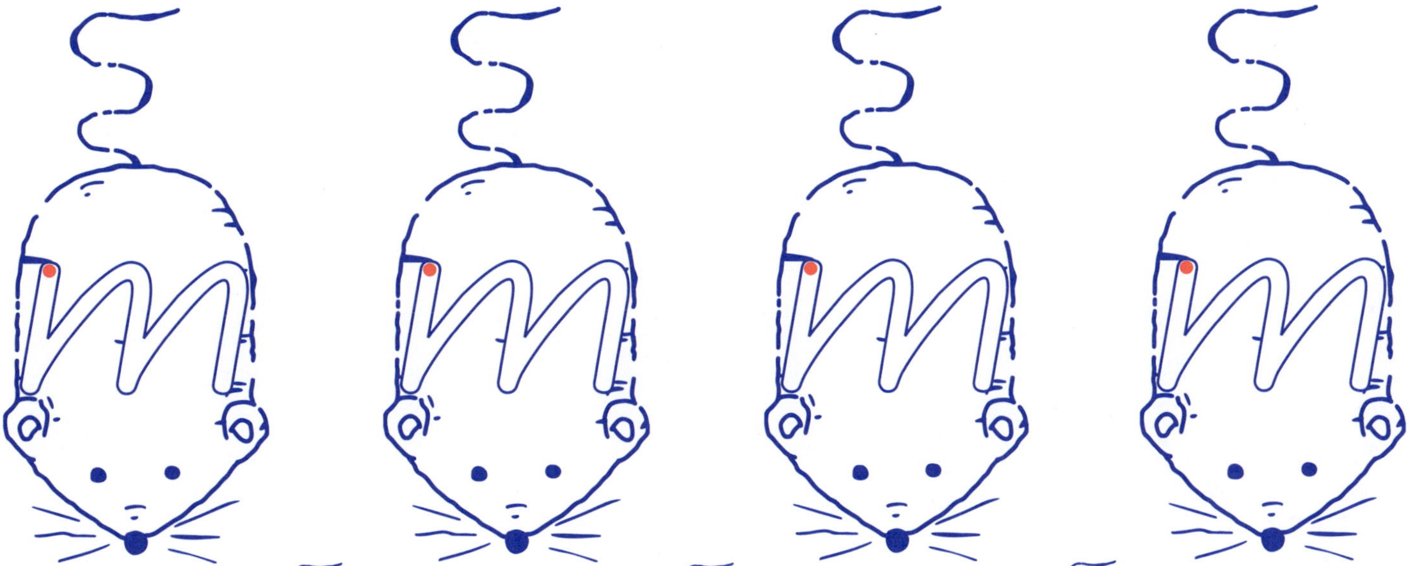

Trace.

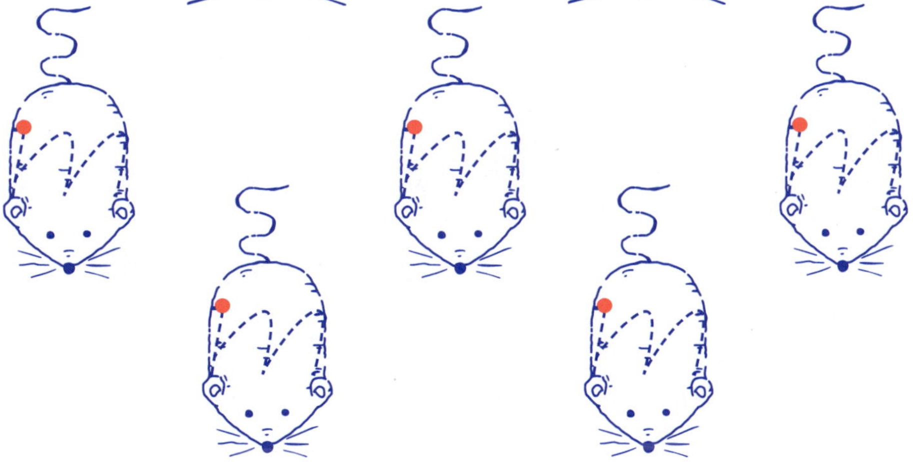

mice

mini mice

Trace.

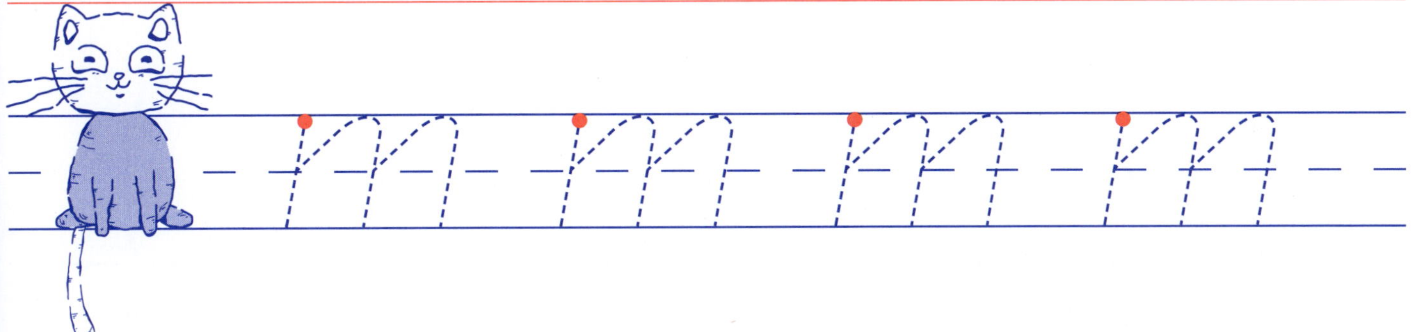

Track. Start at the red dot.

noodles

Trace. Start at the red dot.

nest

Track.

Trace.

Clockwise movement

Track. Start at the red dot.

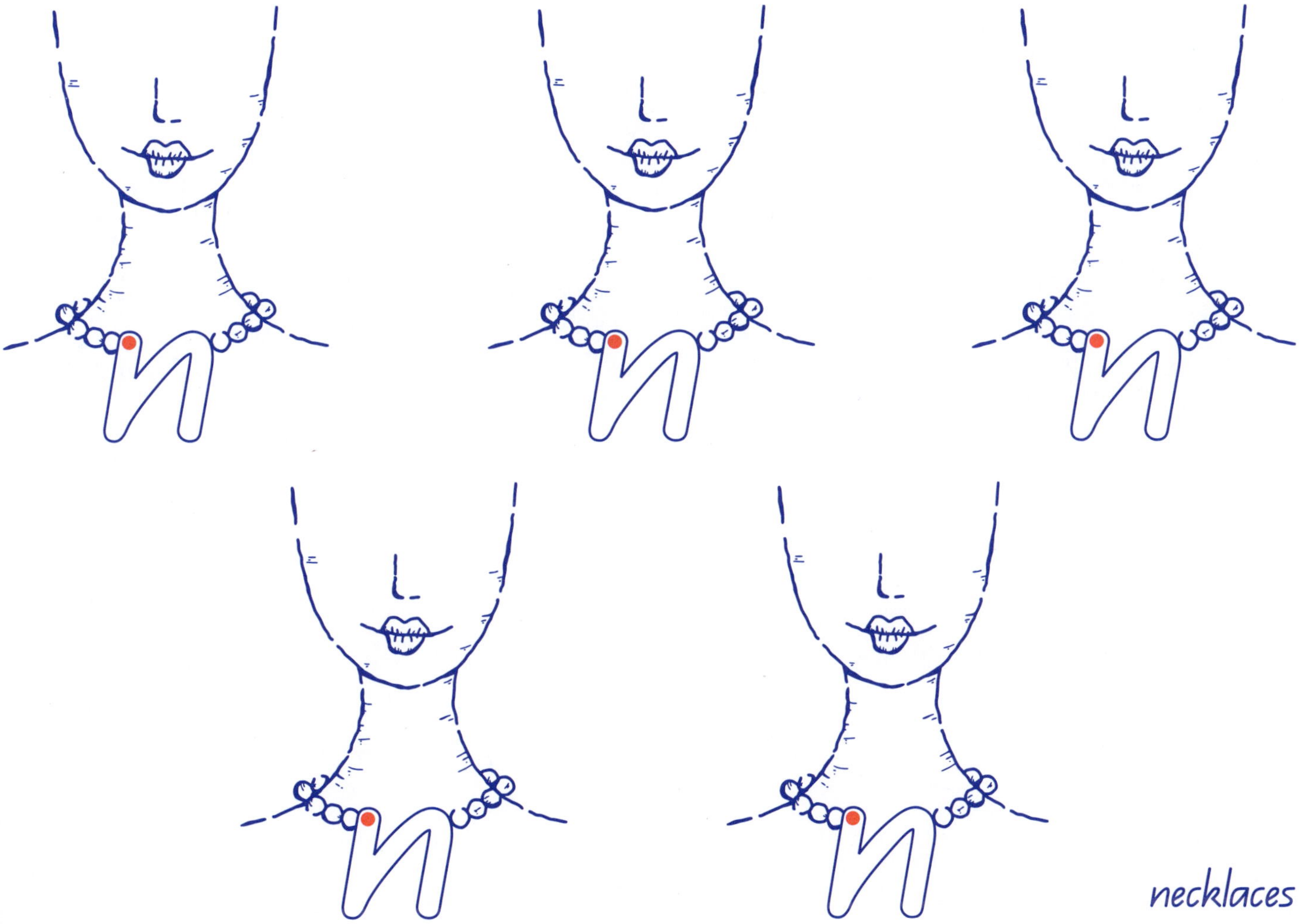

necklaces

Trace.

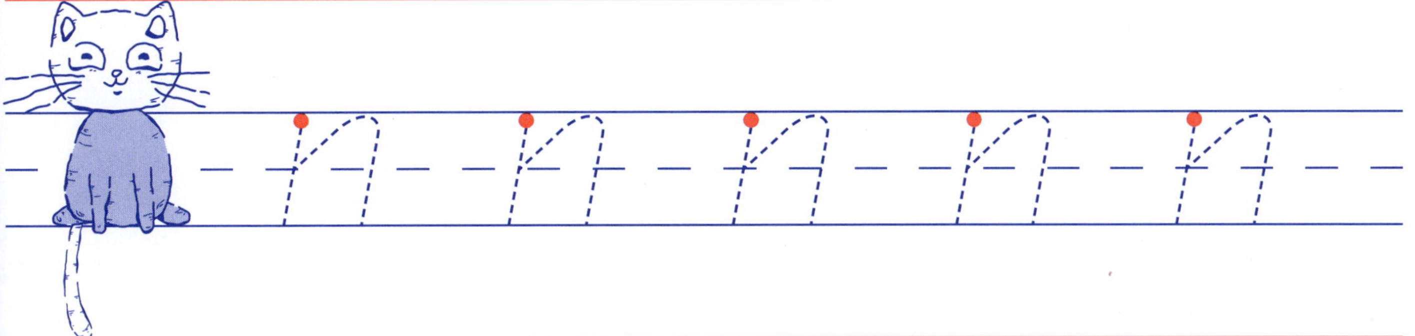

Track. Start at the red dot.

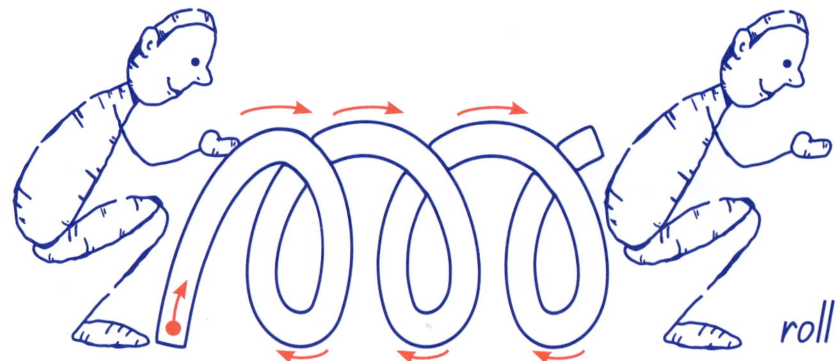

Track. Start at the red dot.

rabbits

Track.

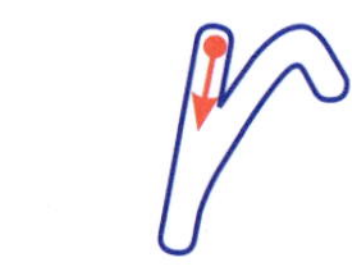

Trace.

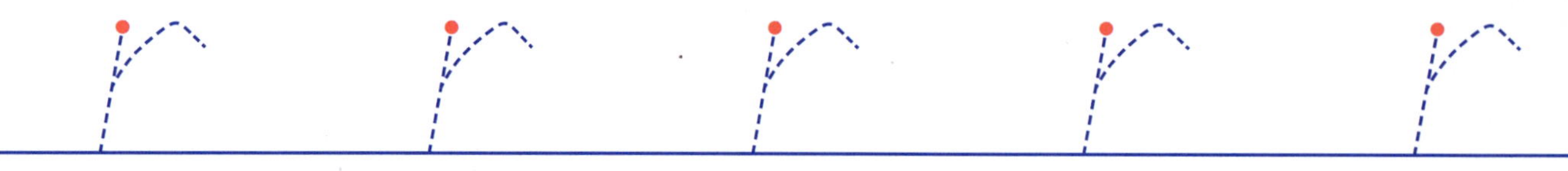

Clockwise movement

Track. Start at the red dot.

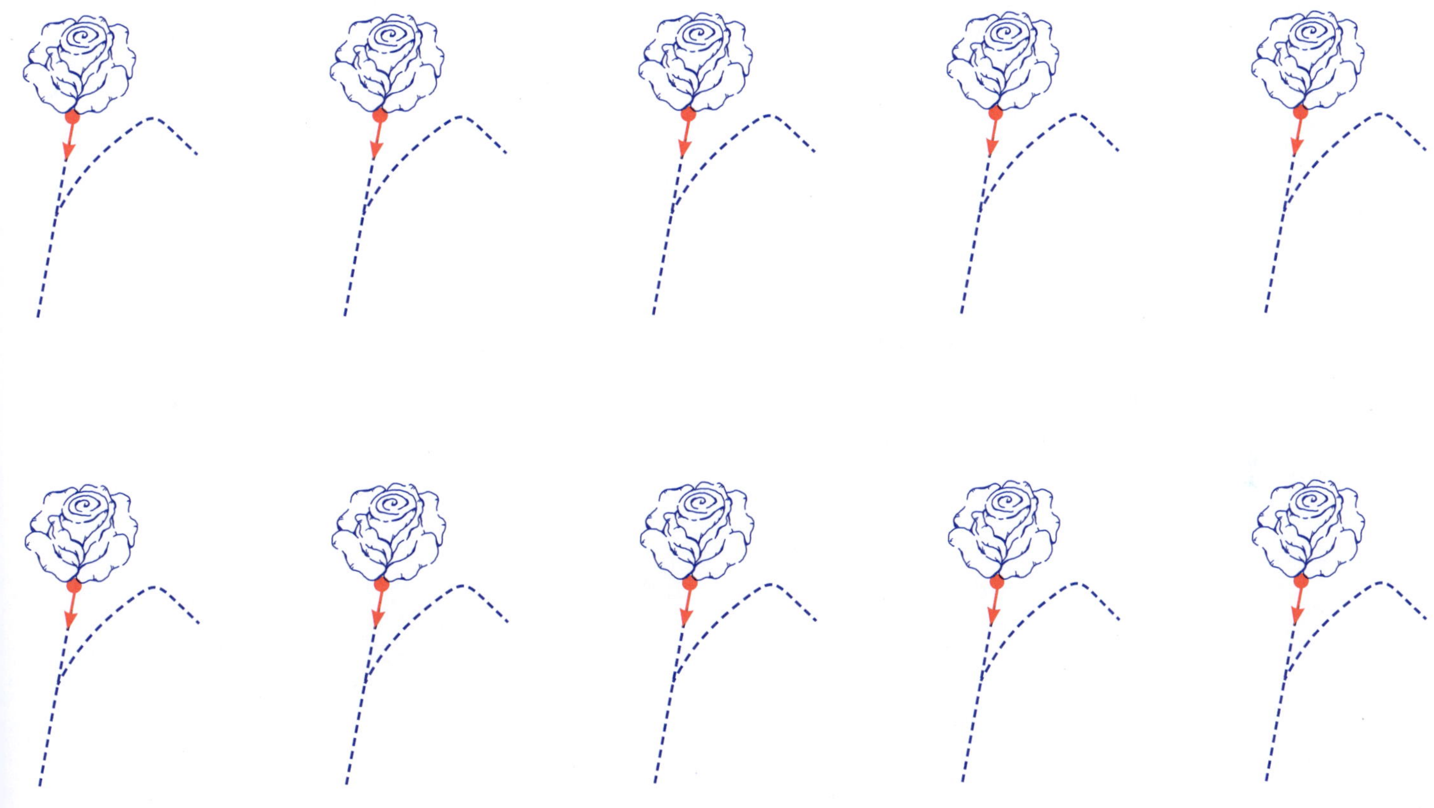

Trace.

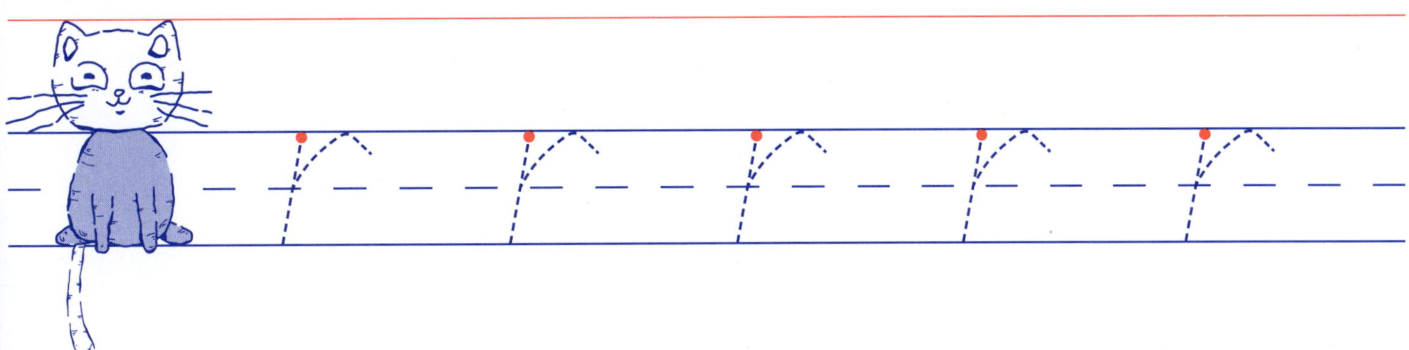

Track. Start at the red dot.

houses

Trace. Start at the red dot.

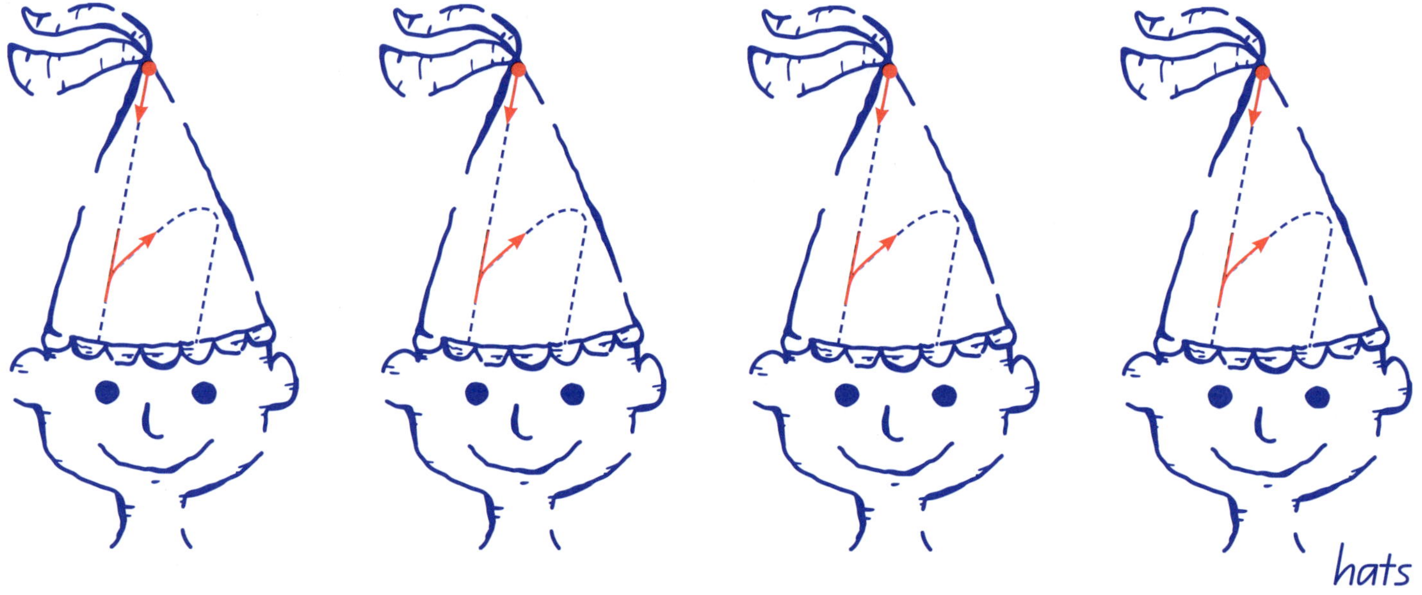

hats

Track.

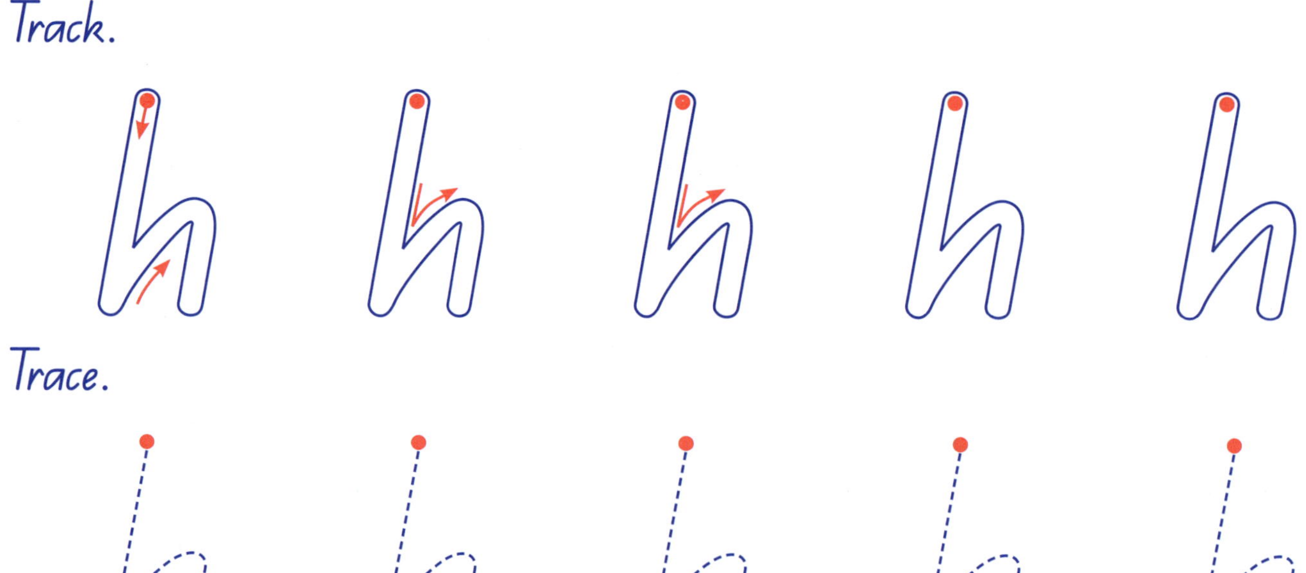

Trace.

Clockwise movement

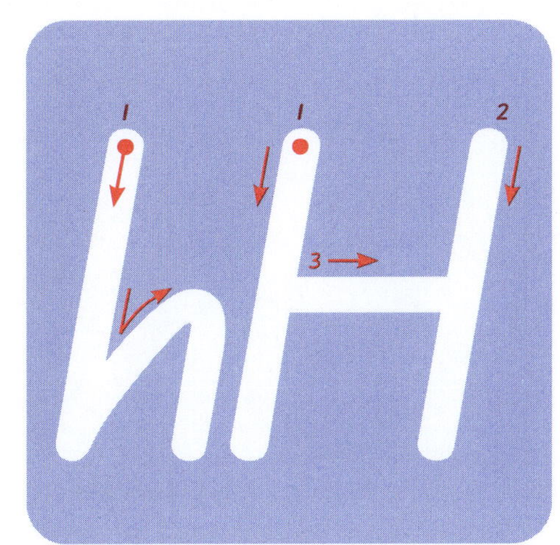

Track. Start at the red dot.

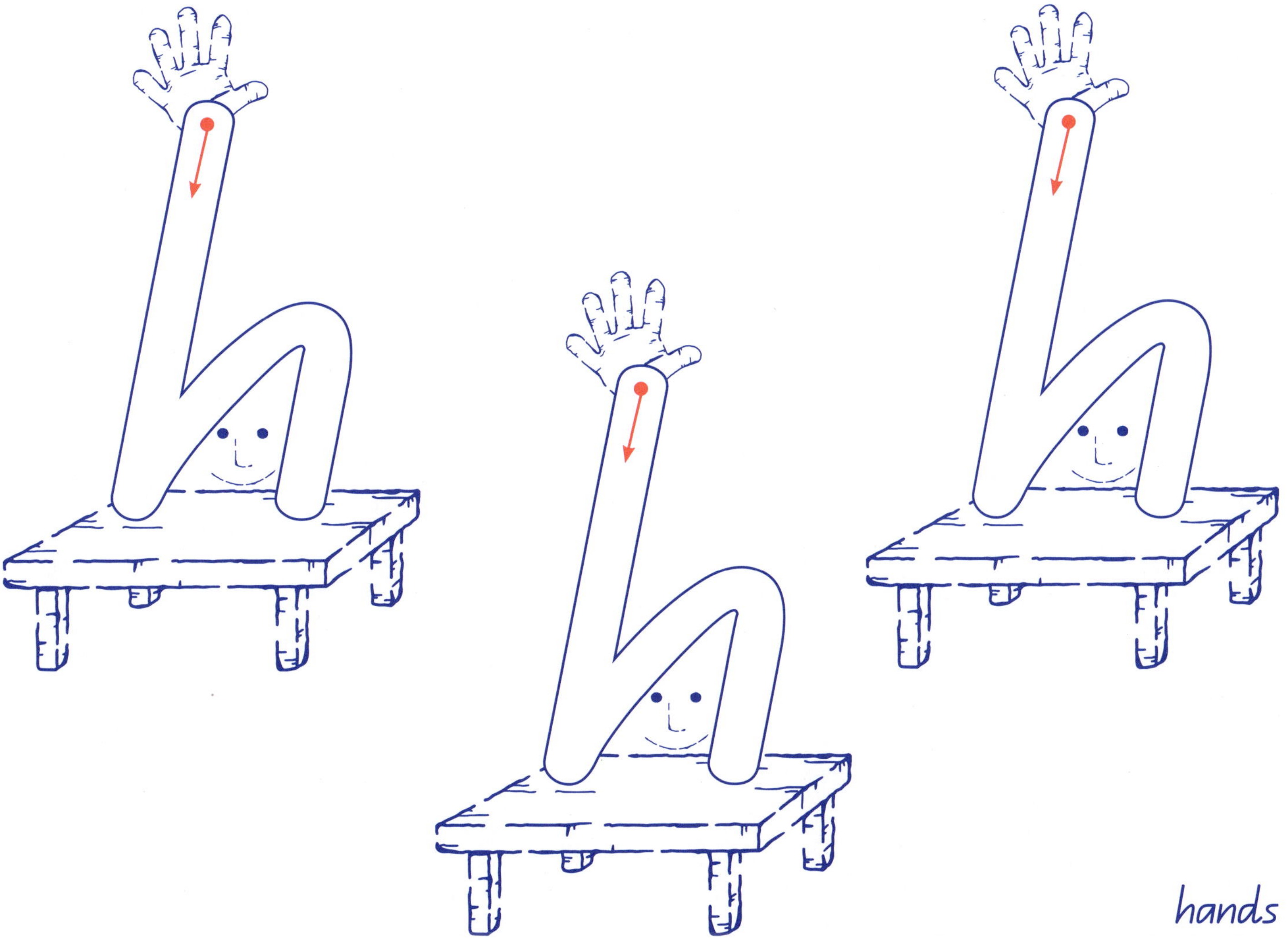

hands

Trace.

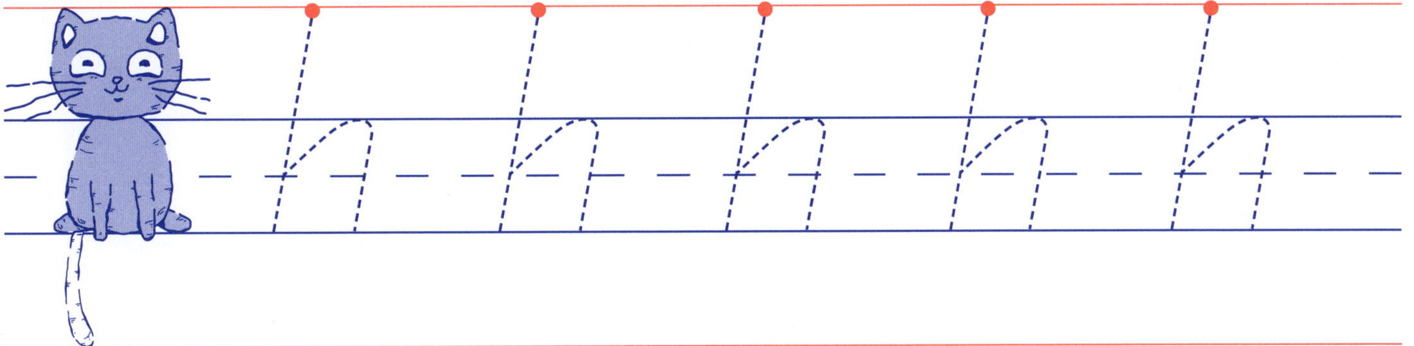

Track. Start at the red dot.

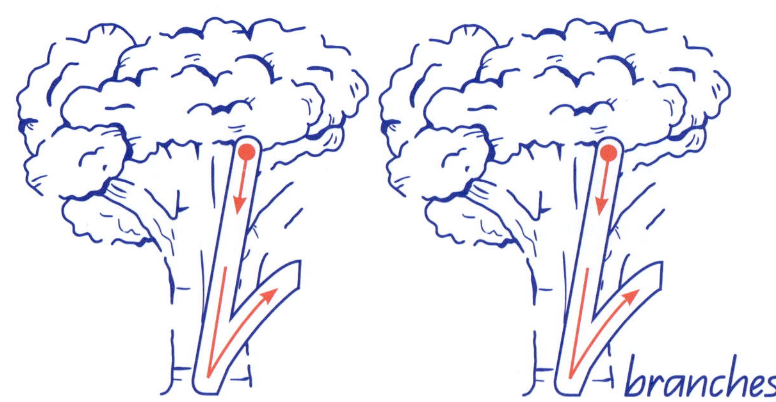

Trace. Start at the red dot.

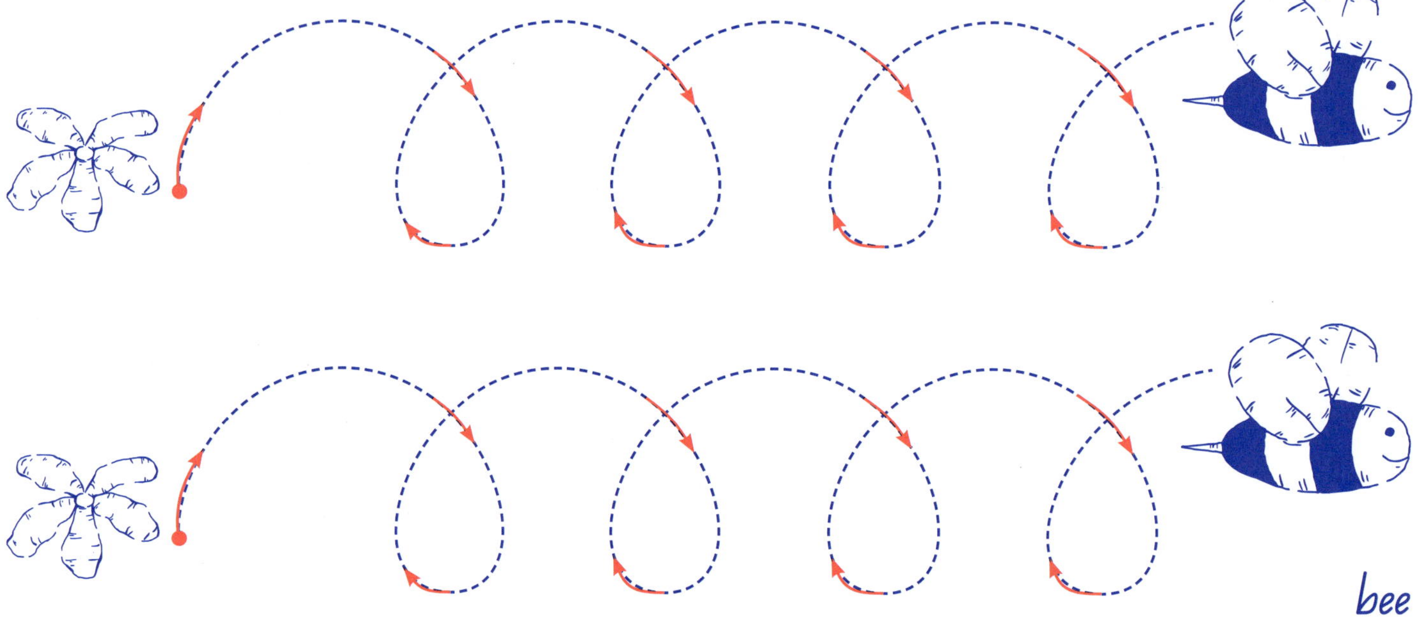

Track.

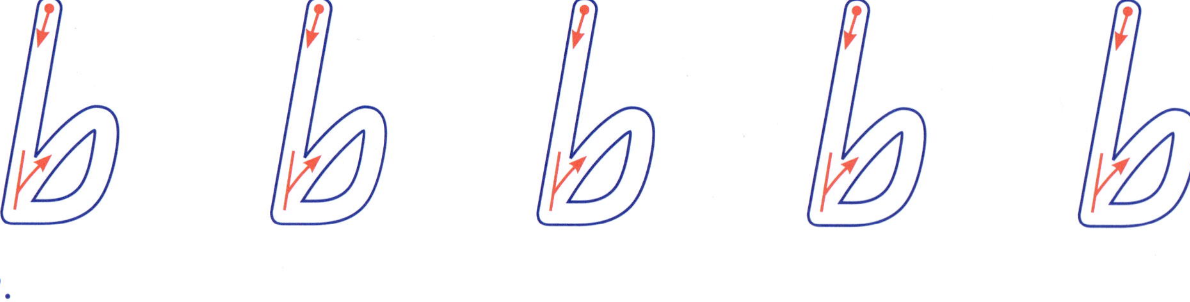

Trace.

Clockwise movement

Track. Start at the red dot.

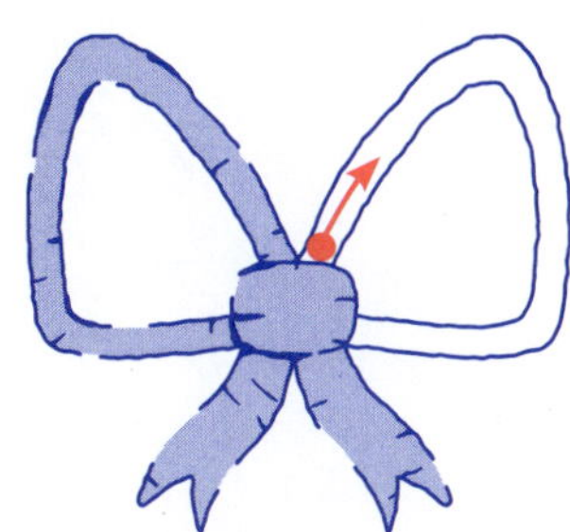
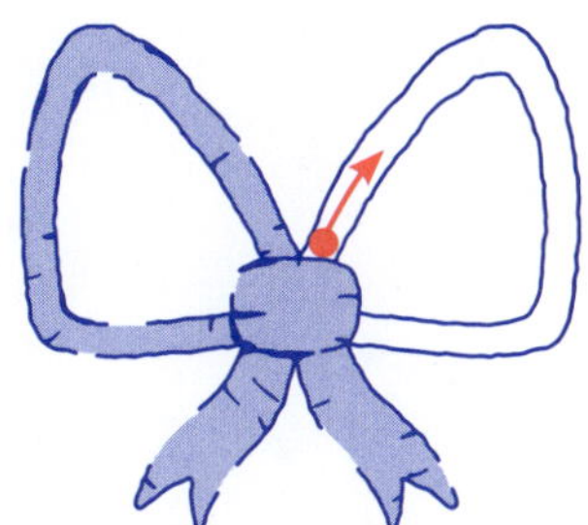
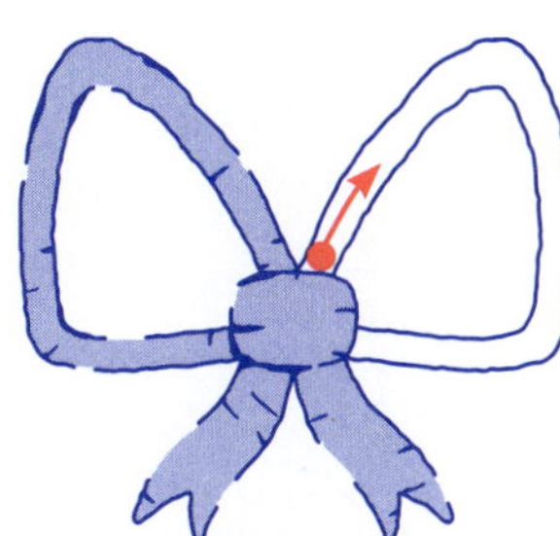
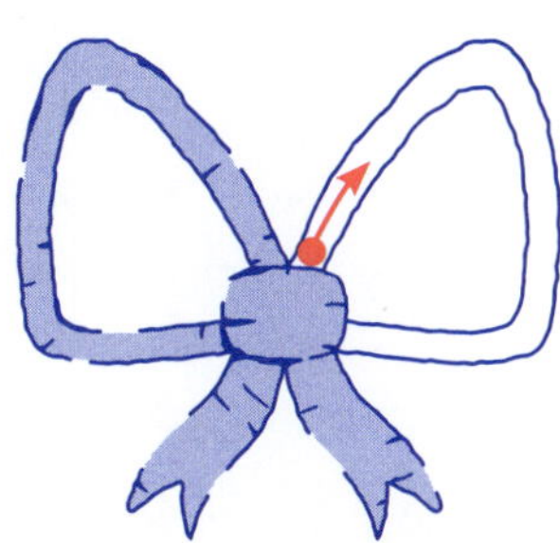

bows

Trace.

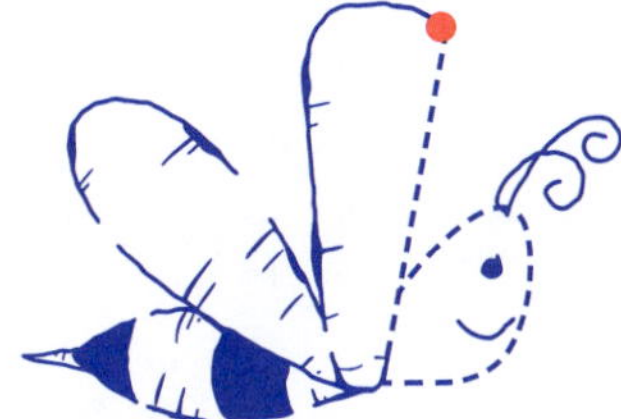
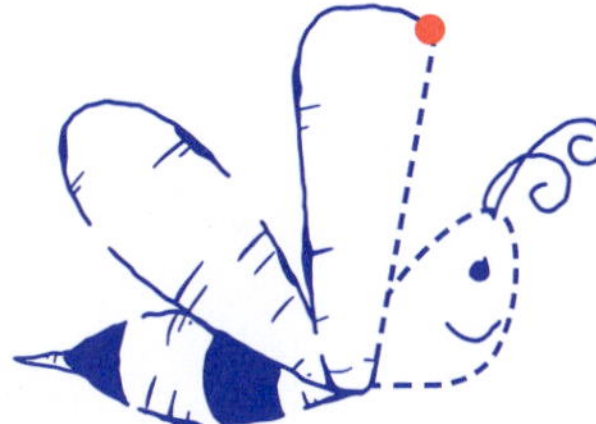

bees

Trace.

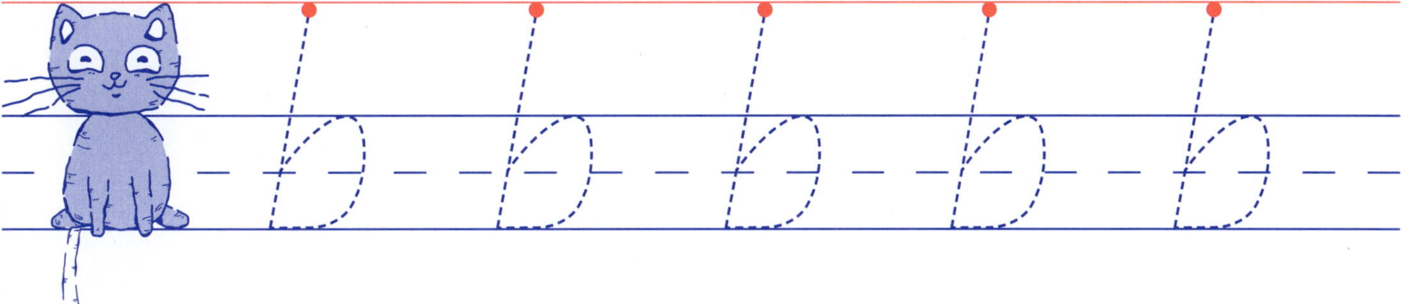

Track. Start at the red dot.

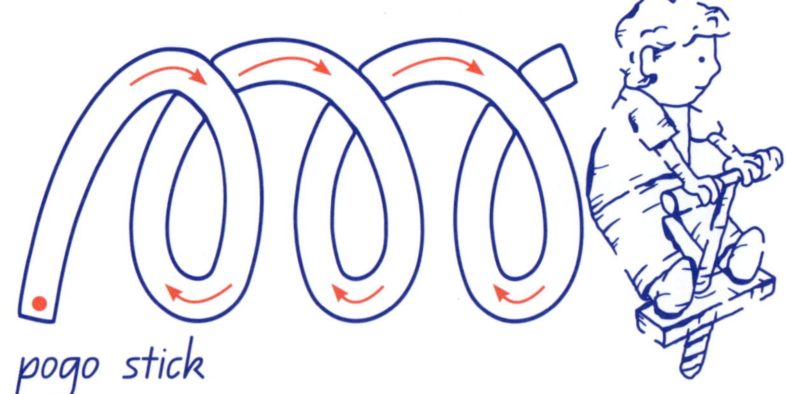

pogo stick

Track.

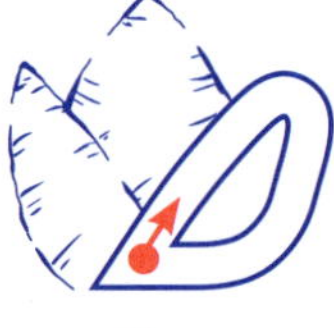
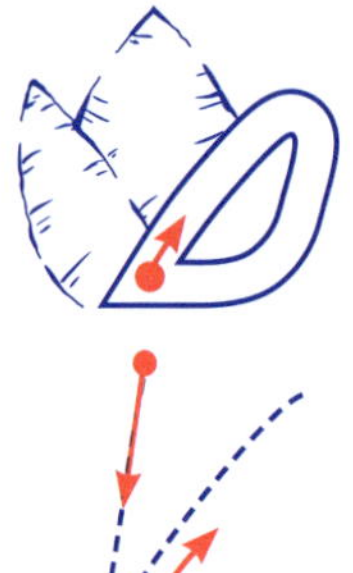
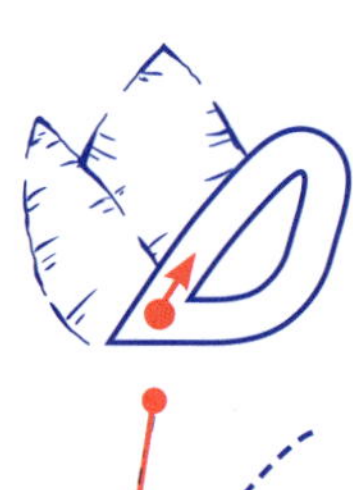
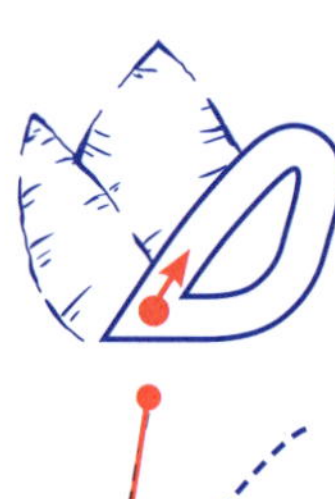

Trace.

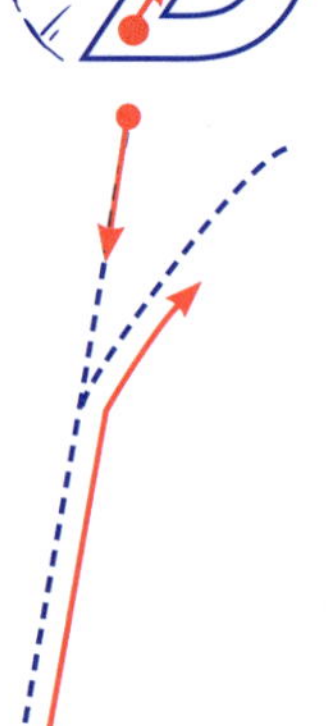
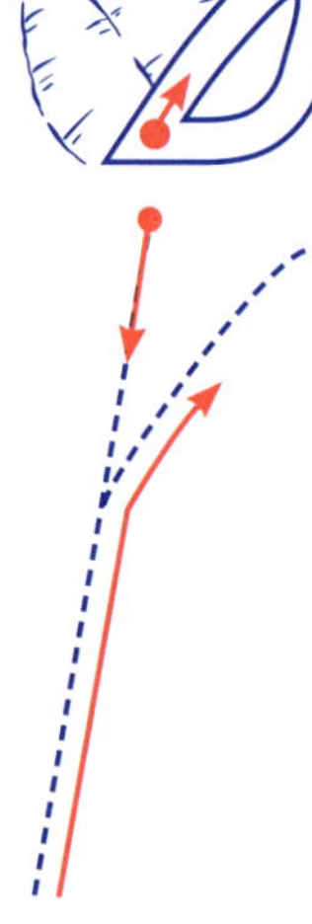
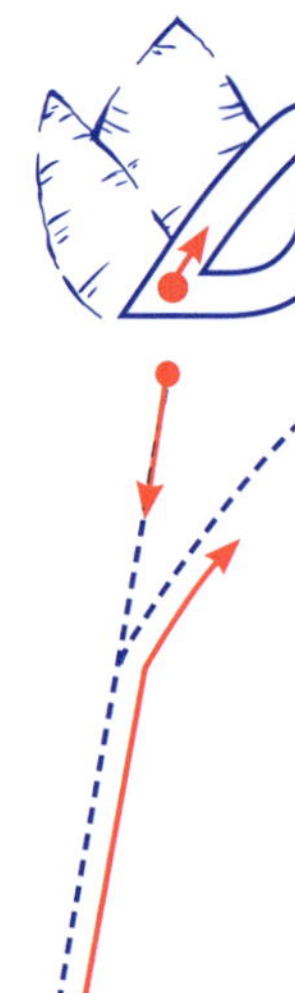

poppies

Track.

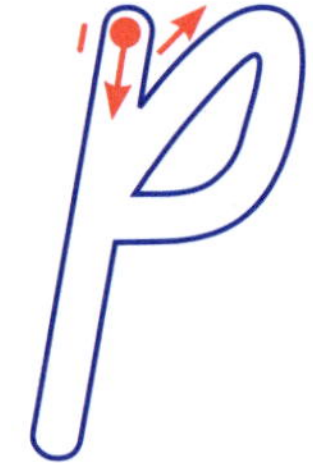

Trace.

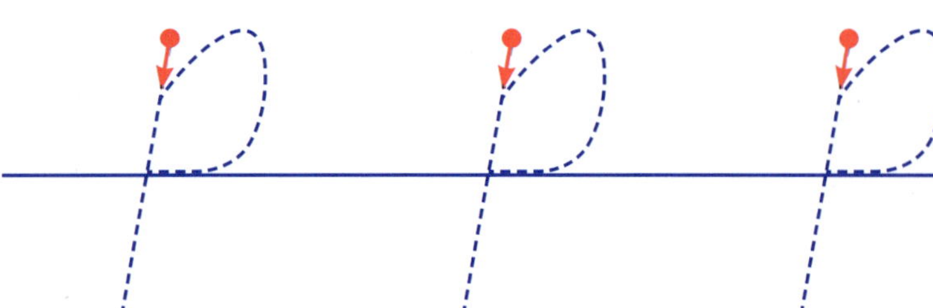

Clockwise movement

Track. Start at the red dot.

parachutes

Trace.

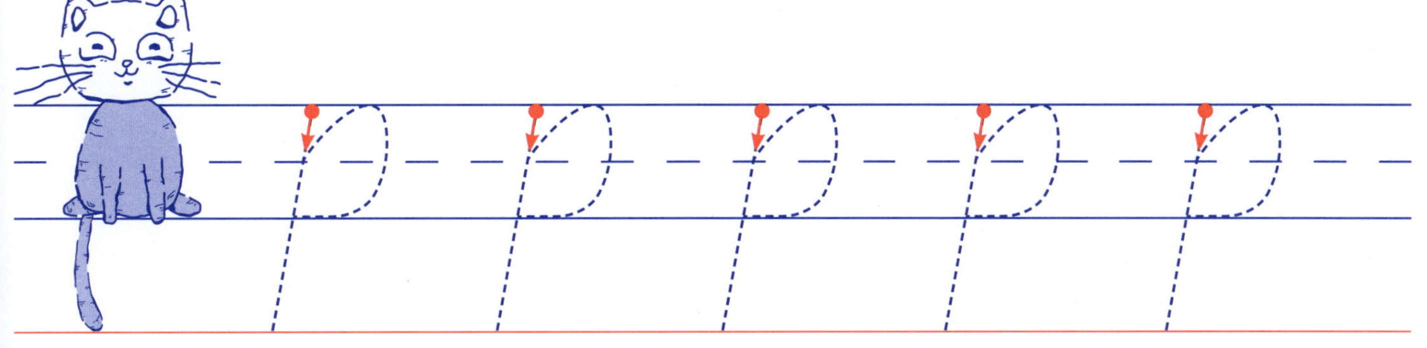

Trace. Start at the red dot.

Track.

Track.

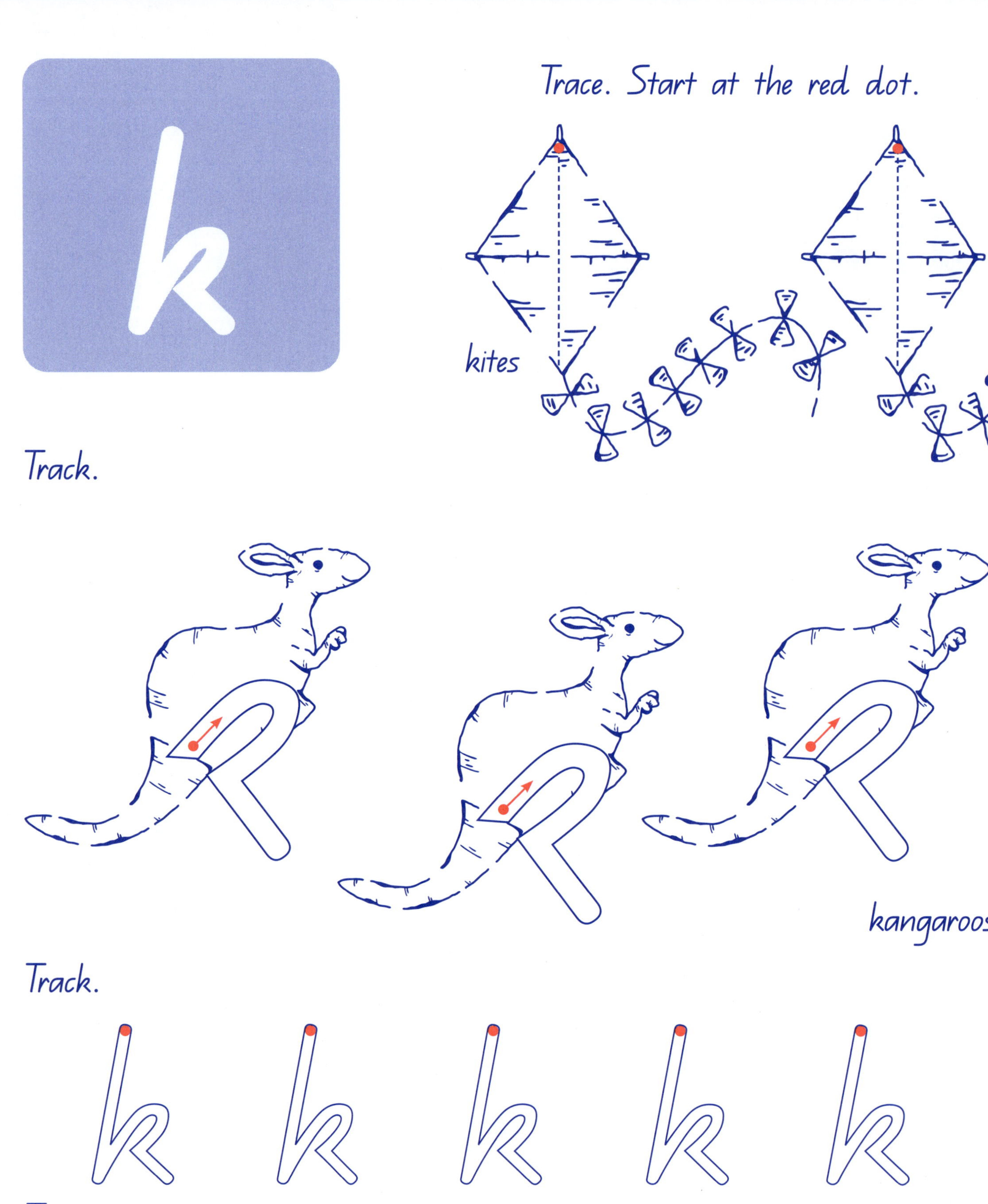

Trace.

Clockwise movement

a head and
body letter

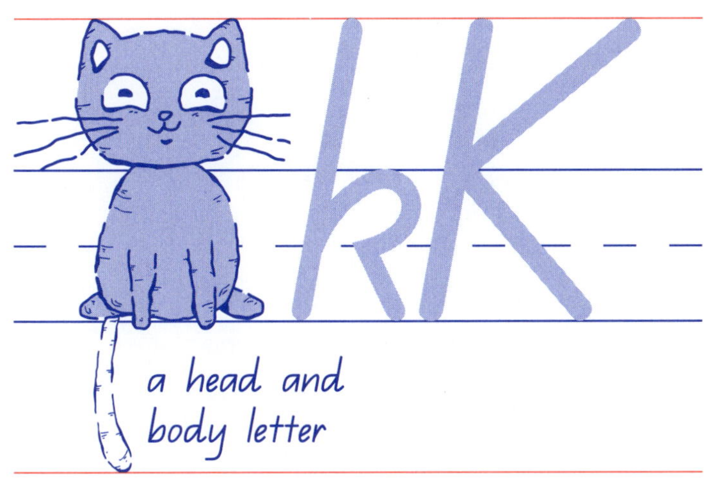

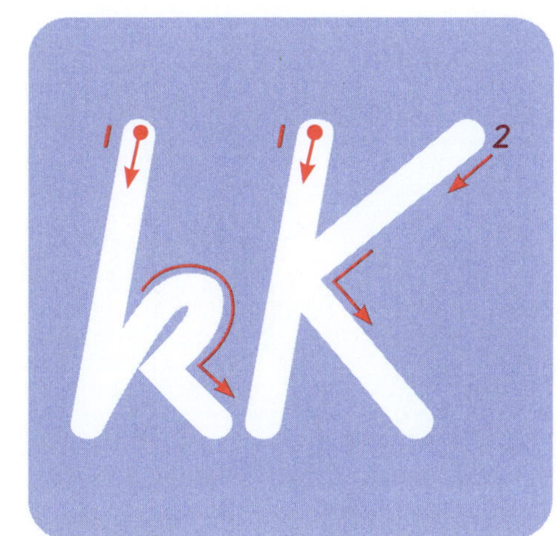

Track. Start at the red dot.

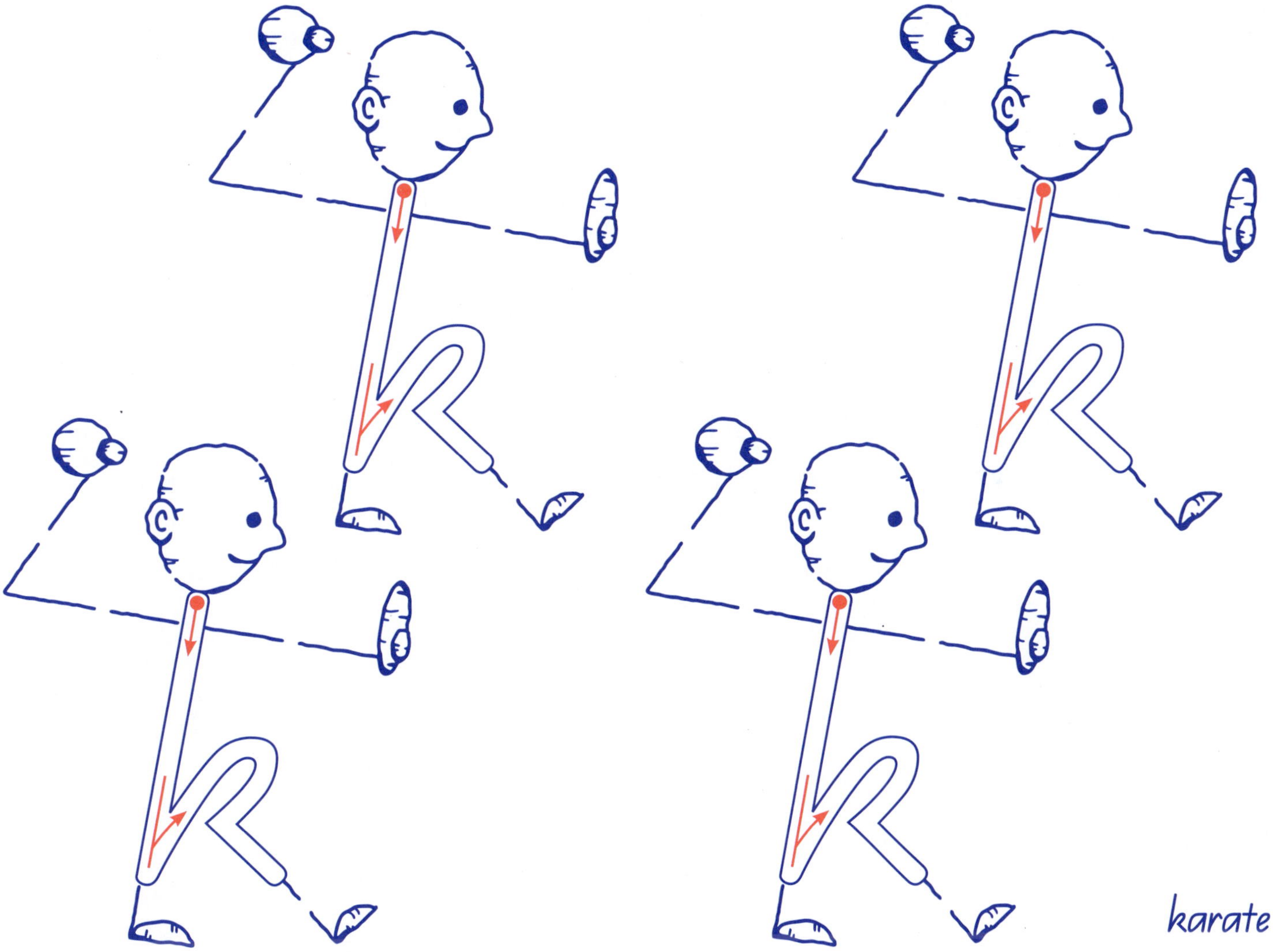

karate

Trace.

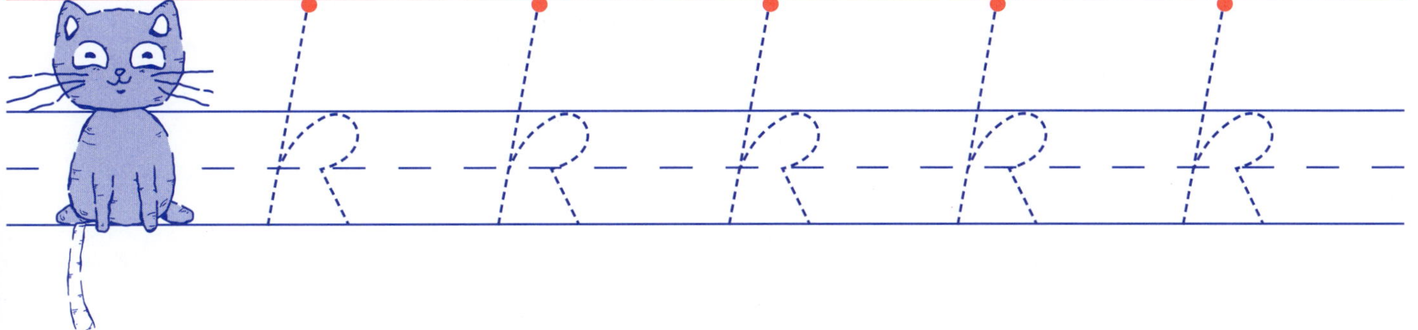

Trace. Start at the red dot.

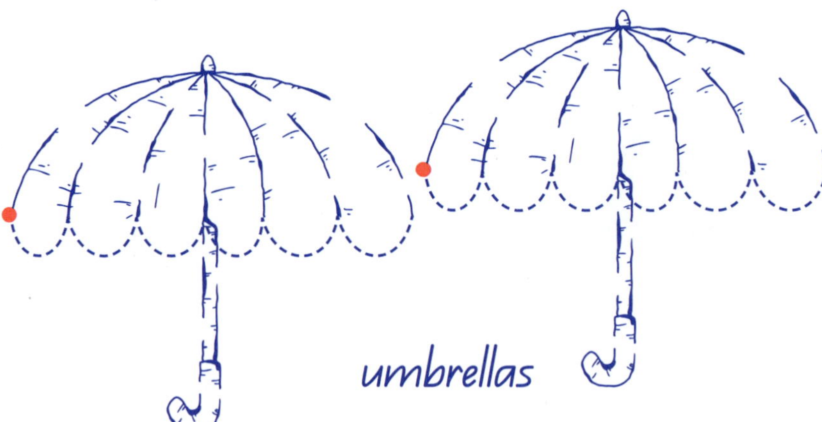

umbrellas

Track. Start at the red dot.

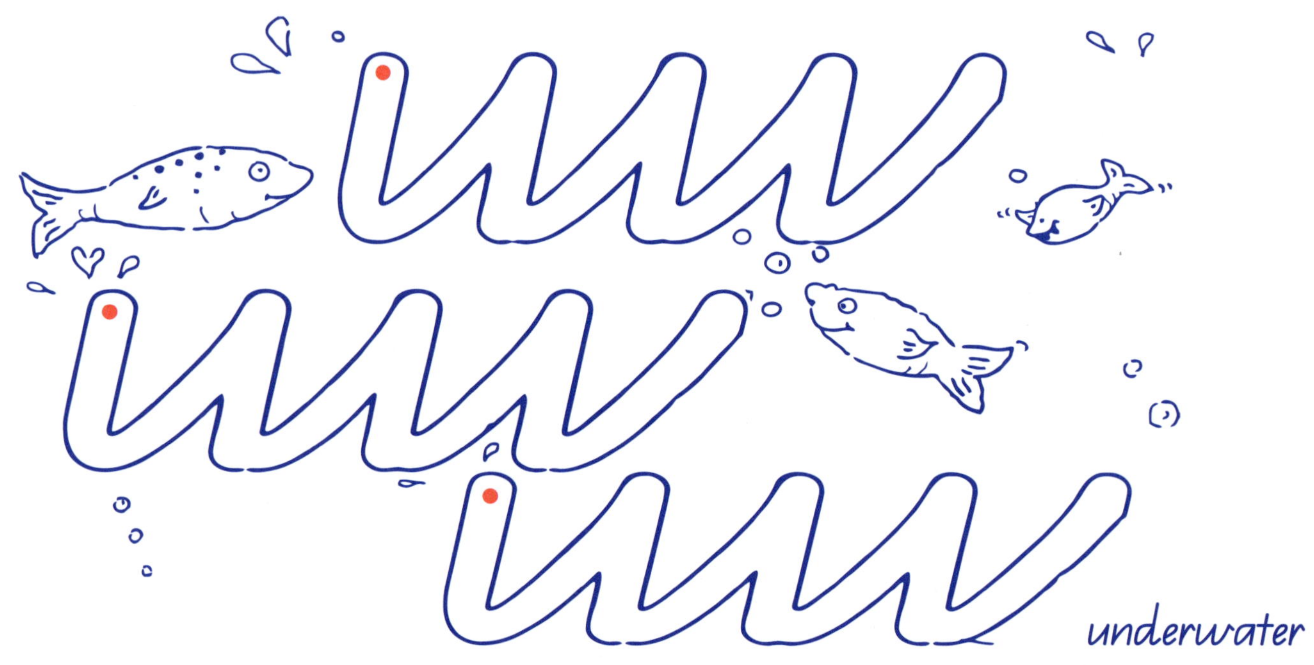

underwater

Track.

Trace.

Anti-clockwise movement

Track. Start at the red dot.

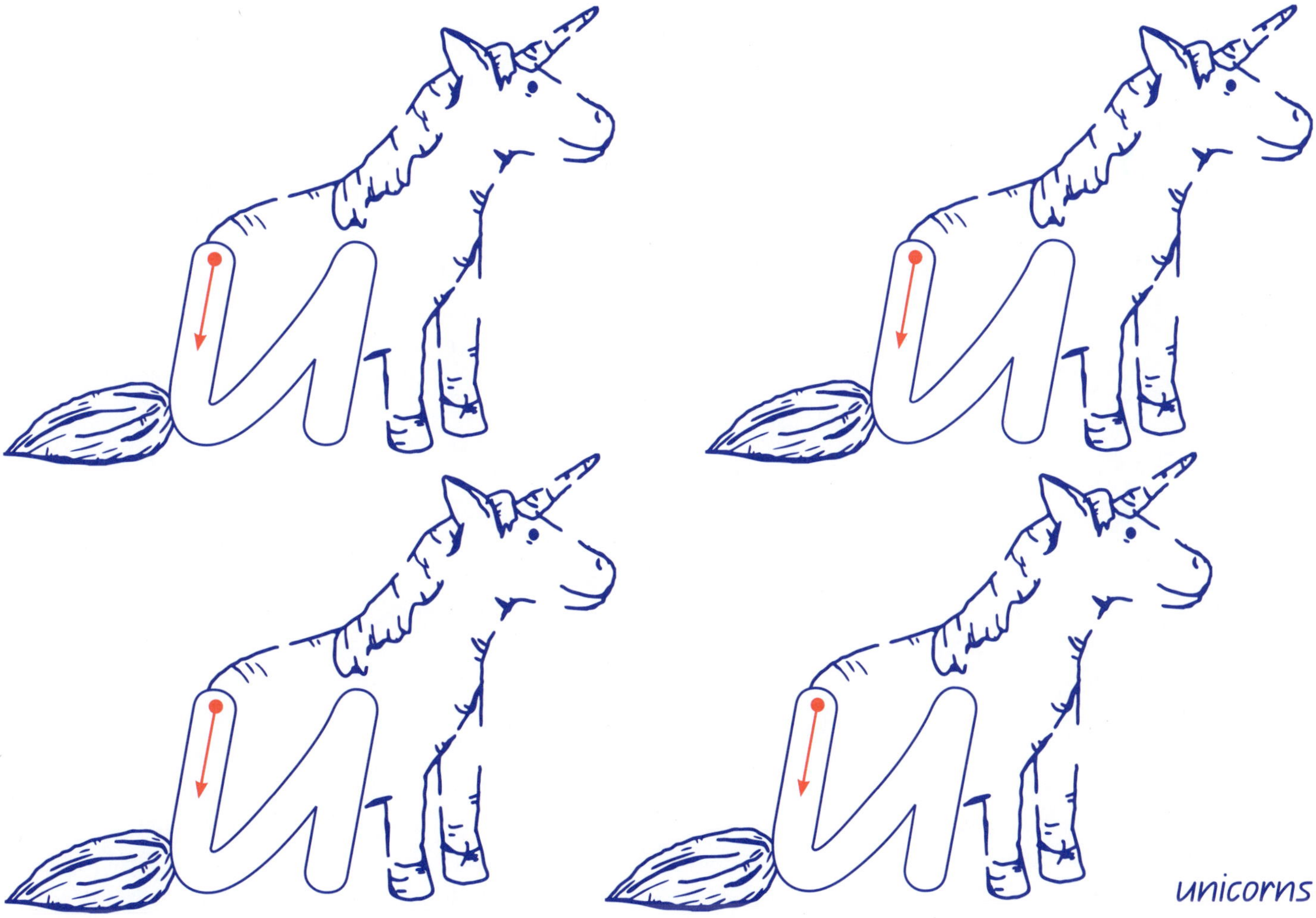

unicorns

Trace.

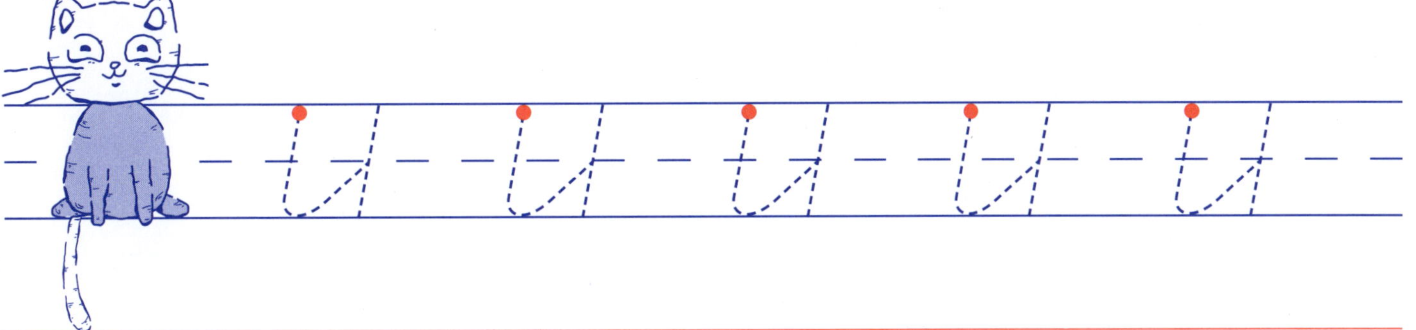

Trace. Start at the red dot.

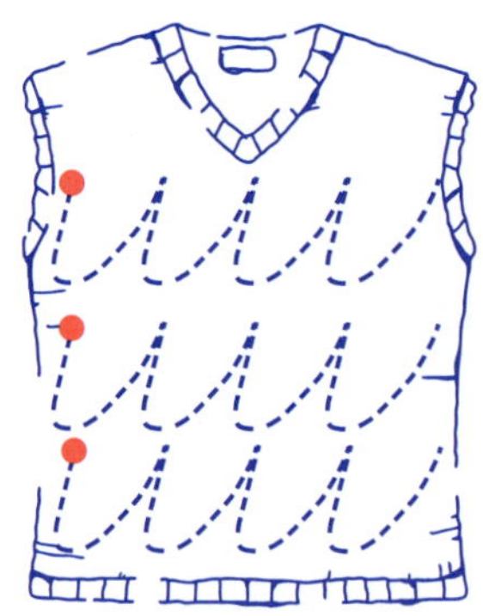

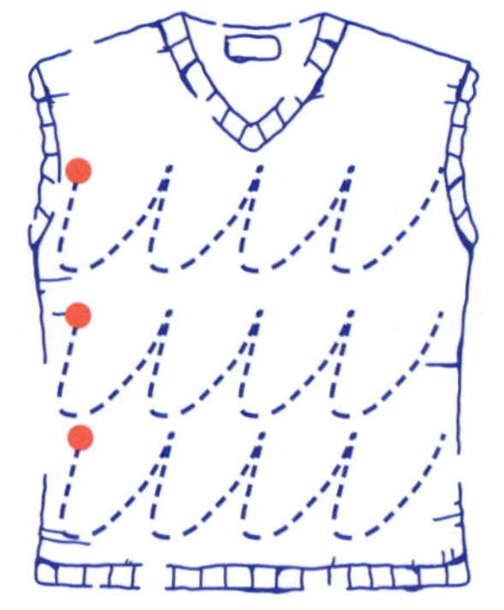

vests

Track. Start at the red dot.

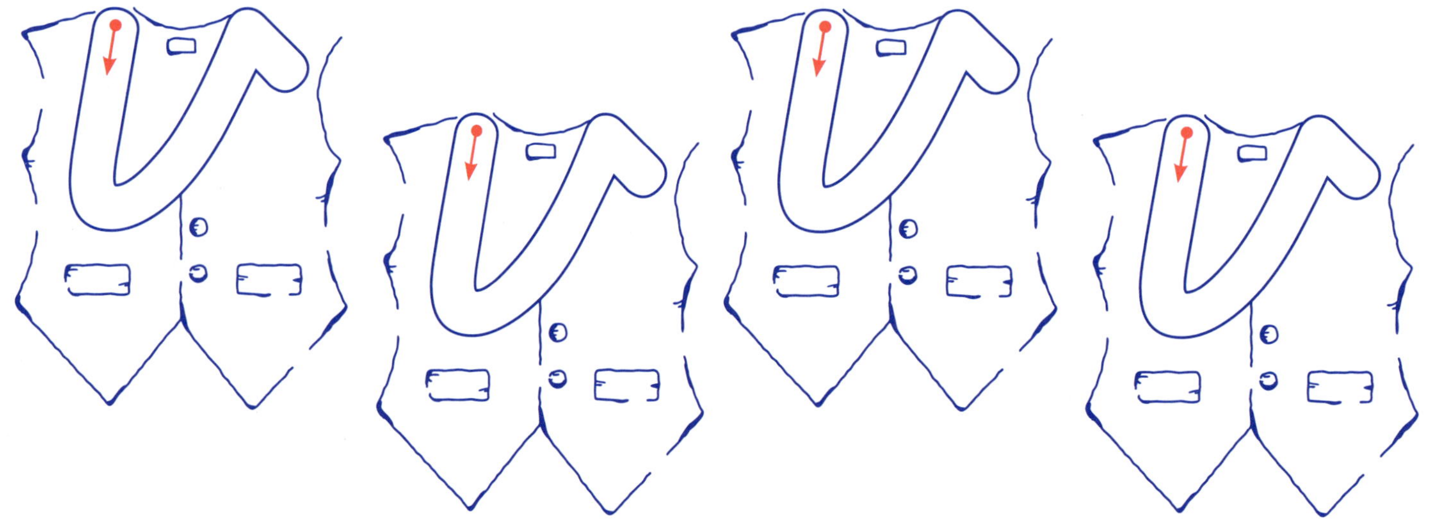

vests

Track.

Trace.

Anti-clockwise movement

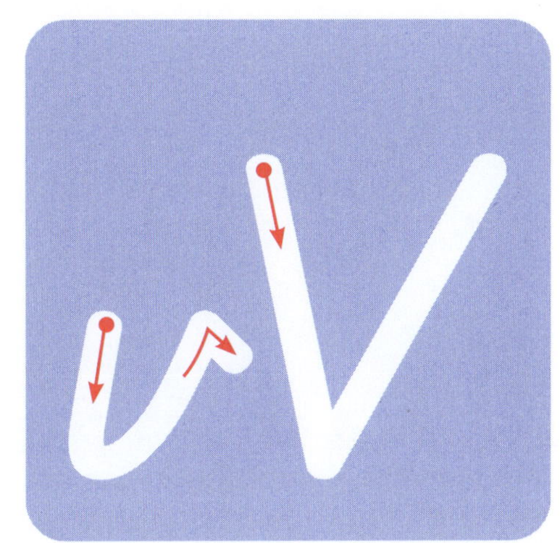

Trace. Start at the red dot.

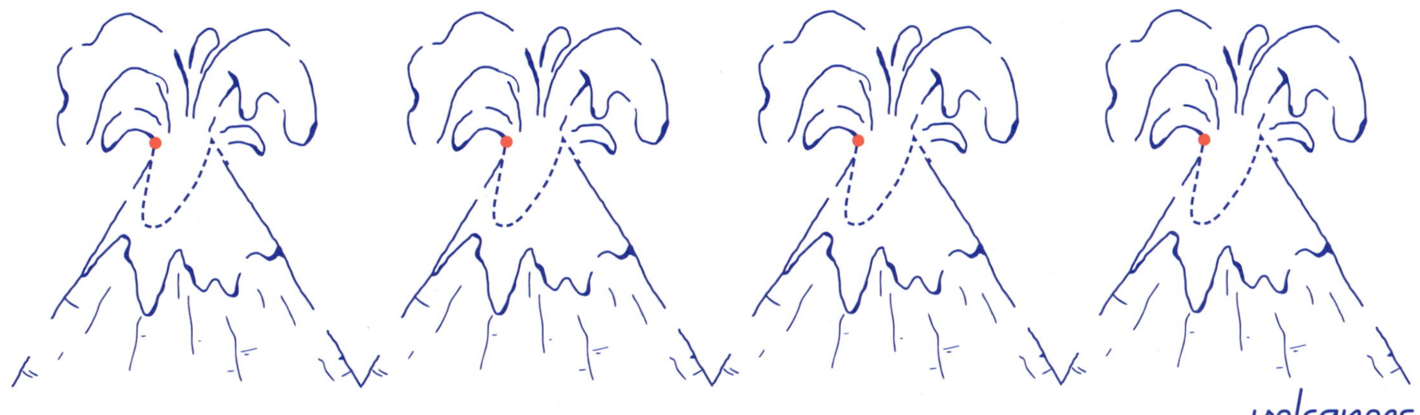

volcanoes

Track.

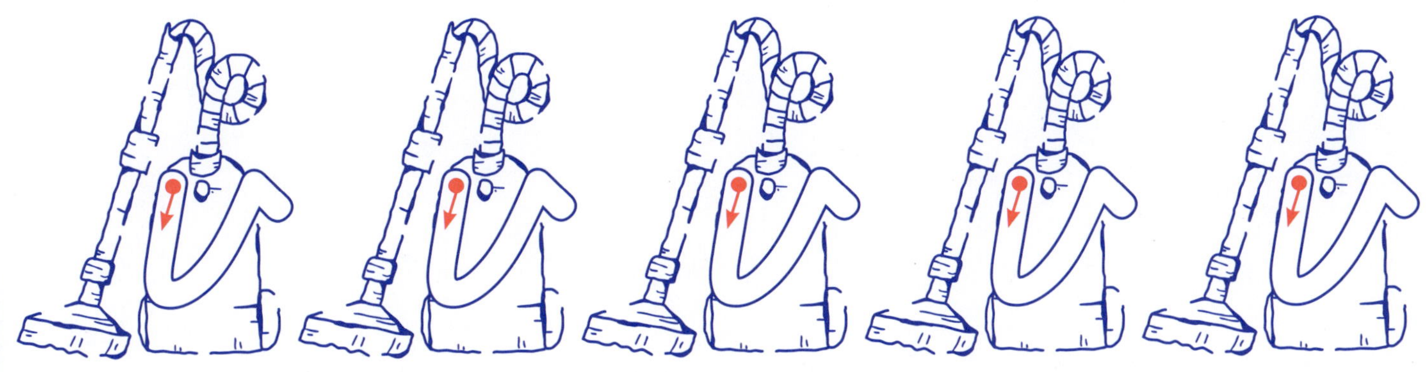

vacuum

Trace.

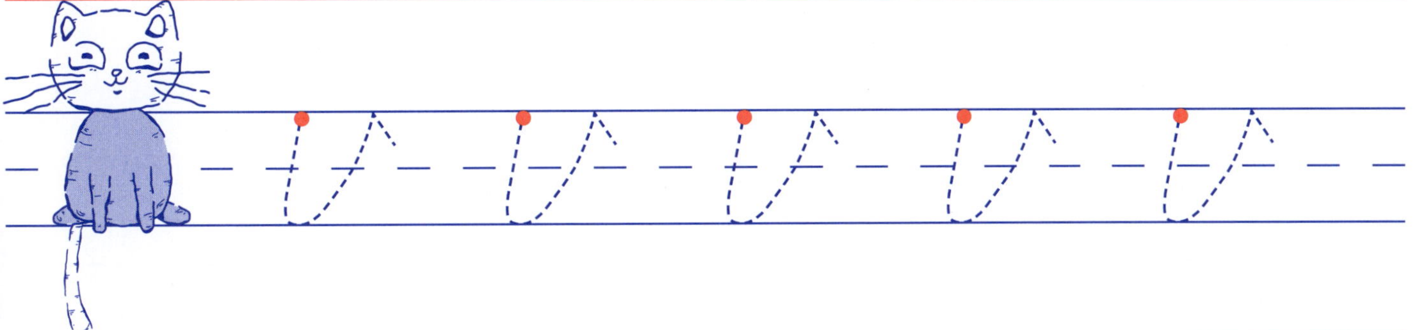

Track. Start at the red dot.

whale

Trace. Start at the red dot.

waves

Track.

Trace.

Anti-clockwise movement

a body letter

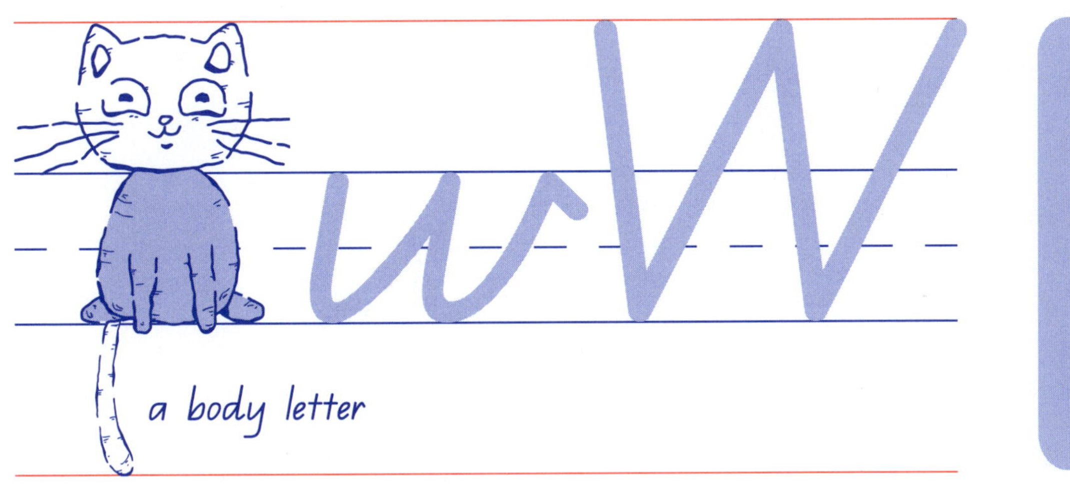

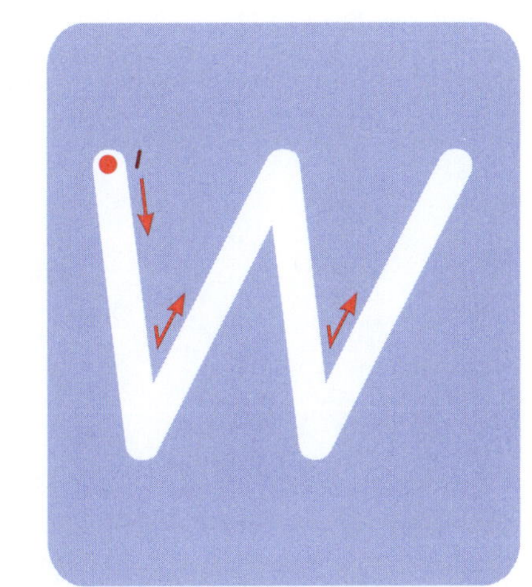

Track. Start at the red dot.

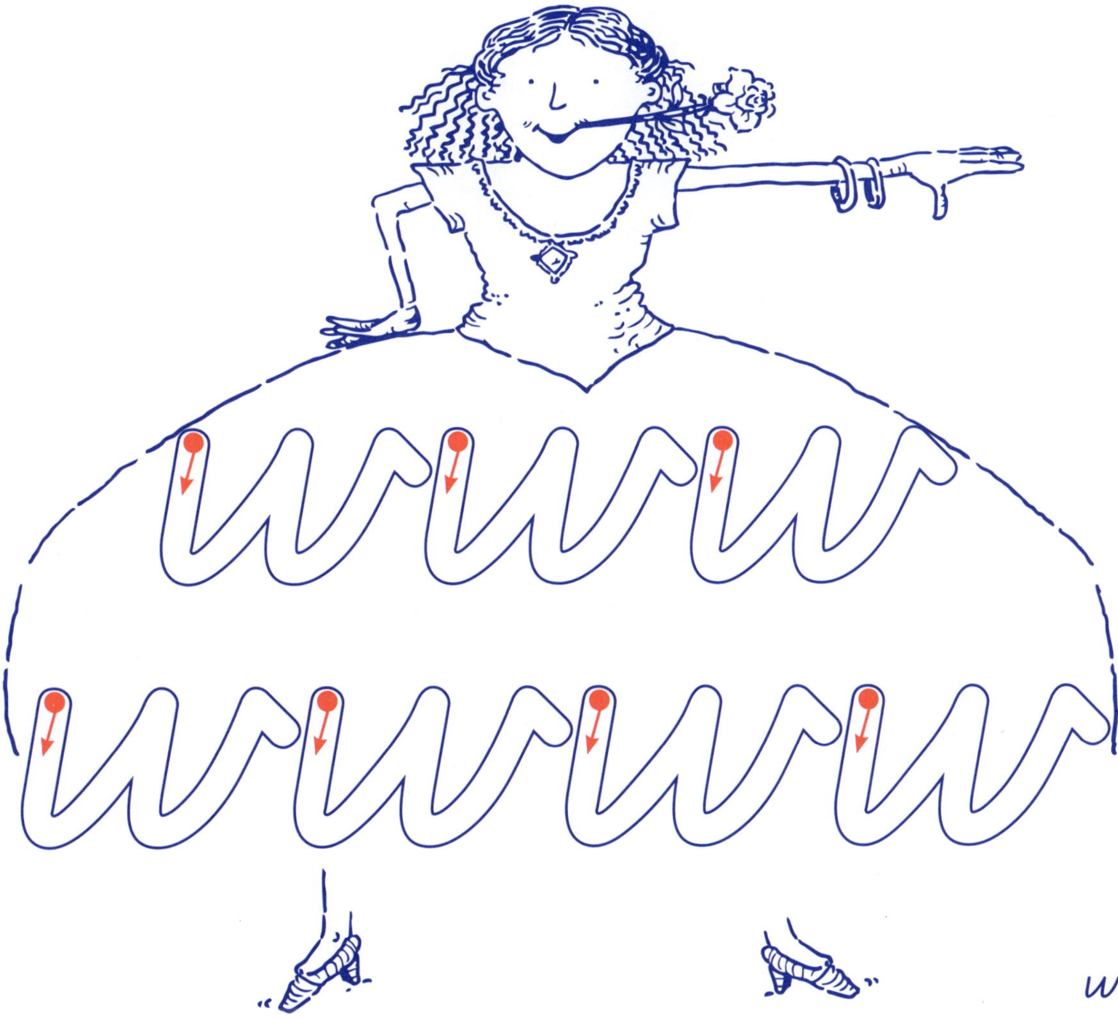

woman

Trace.

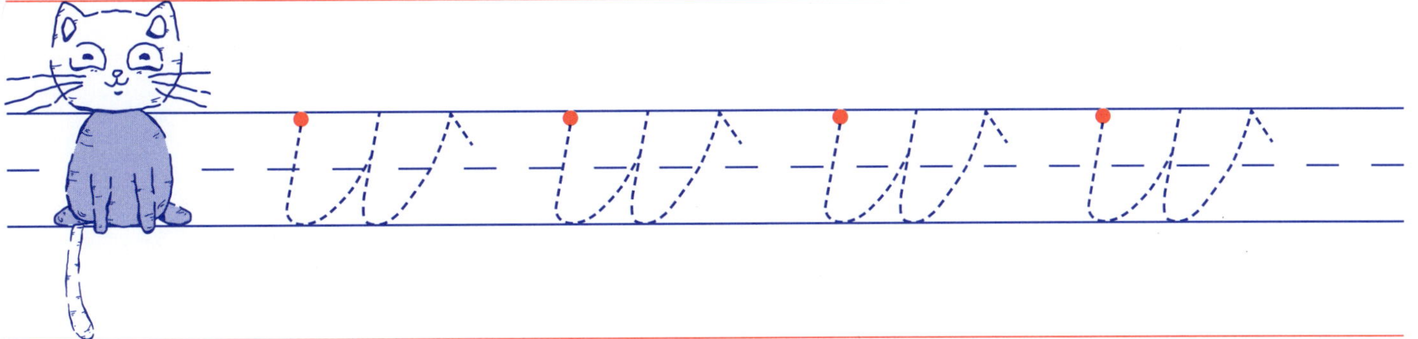

Trace. Start at the red dot.

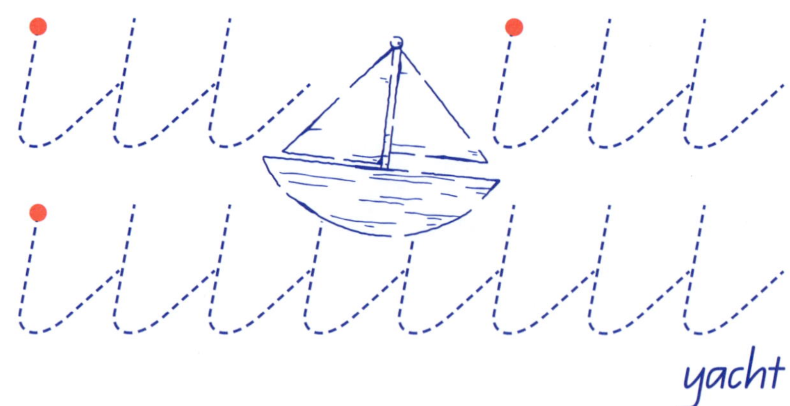

yacht

Track. Start at the red dot.

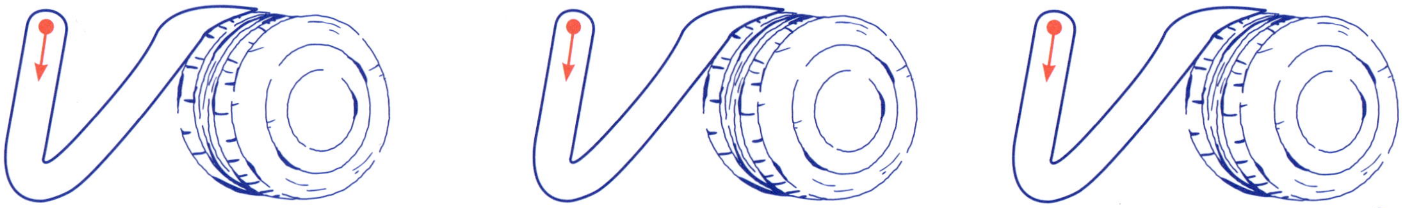

yoyo's

yoghurt

Track.

Trace.

Anti-clockwise movement

a body and
tail letter

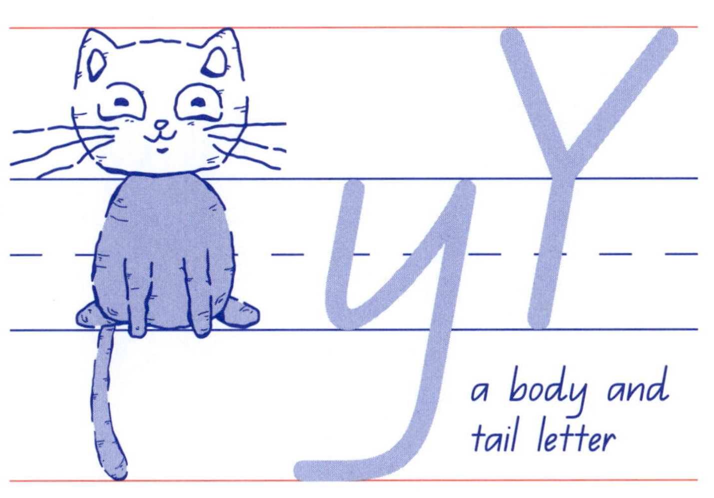

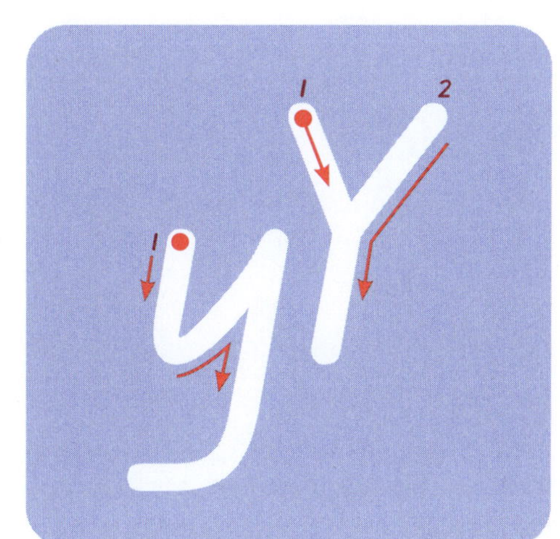

Track. Start at the red dot.

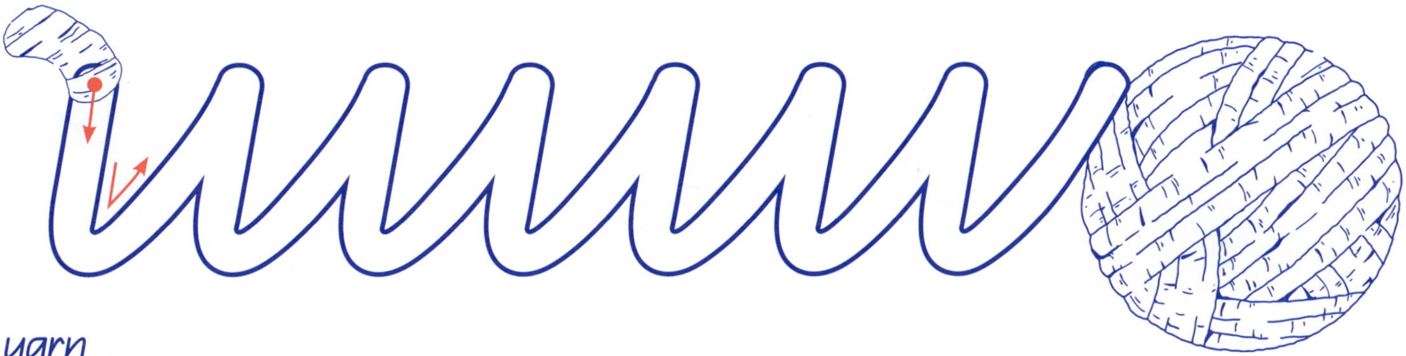

yarn

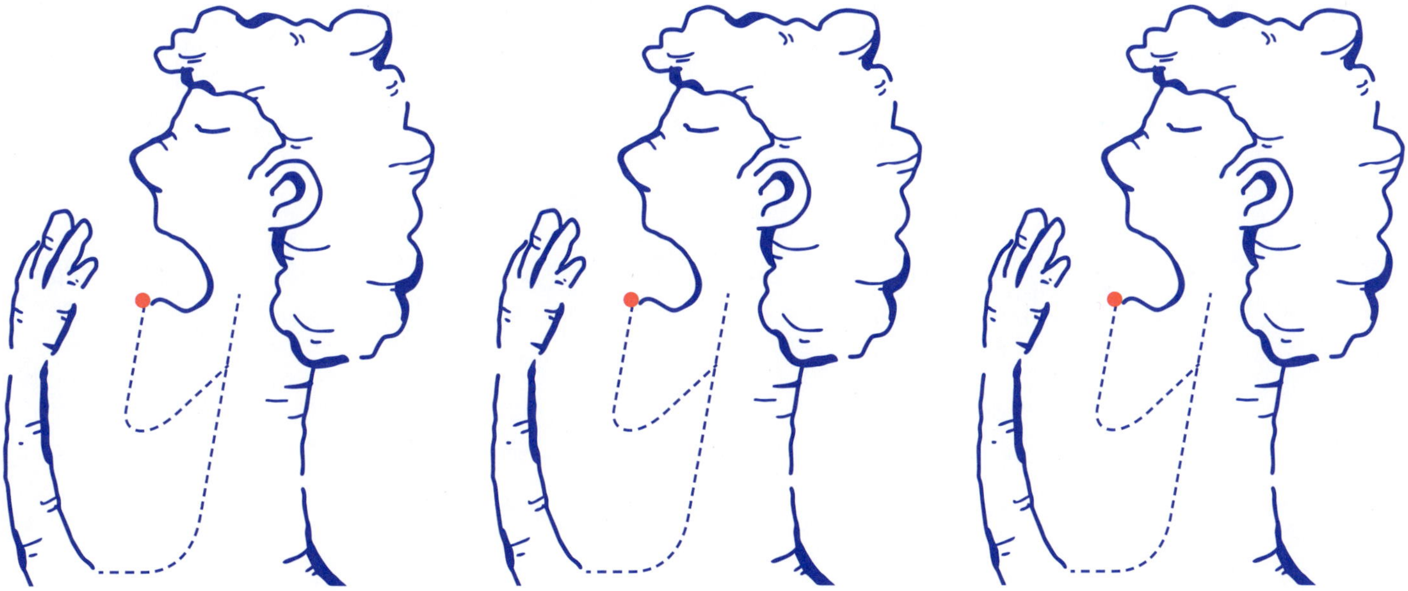

yawns

Trace.

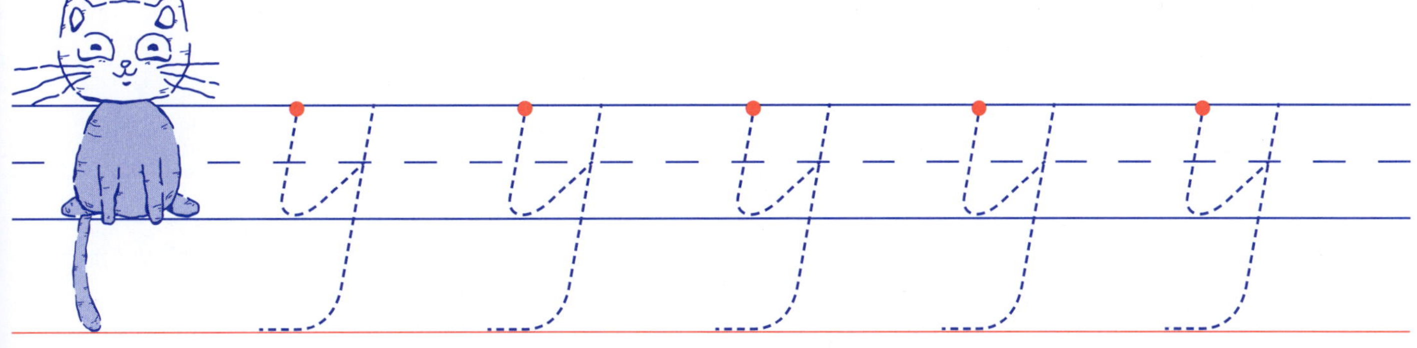

Trace. Start at the red dot.

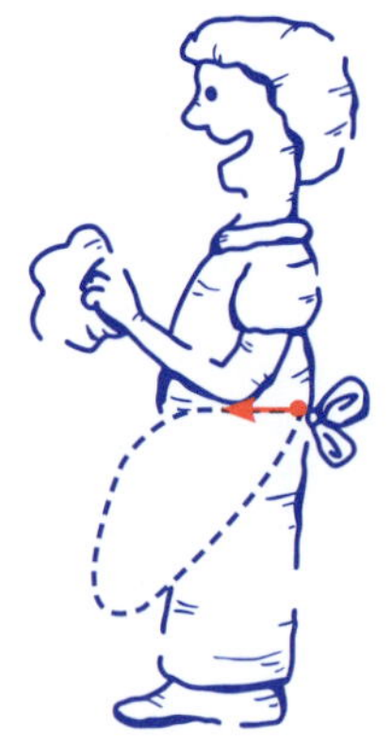

Track.

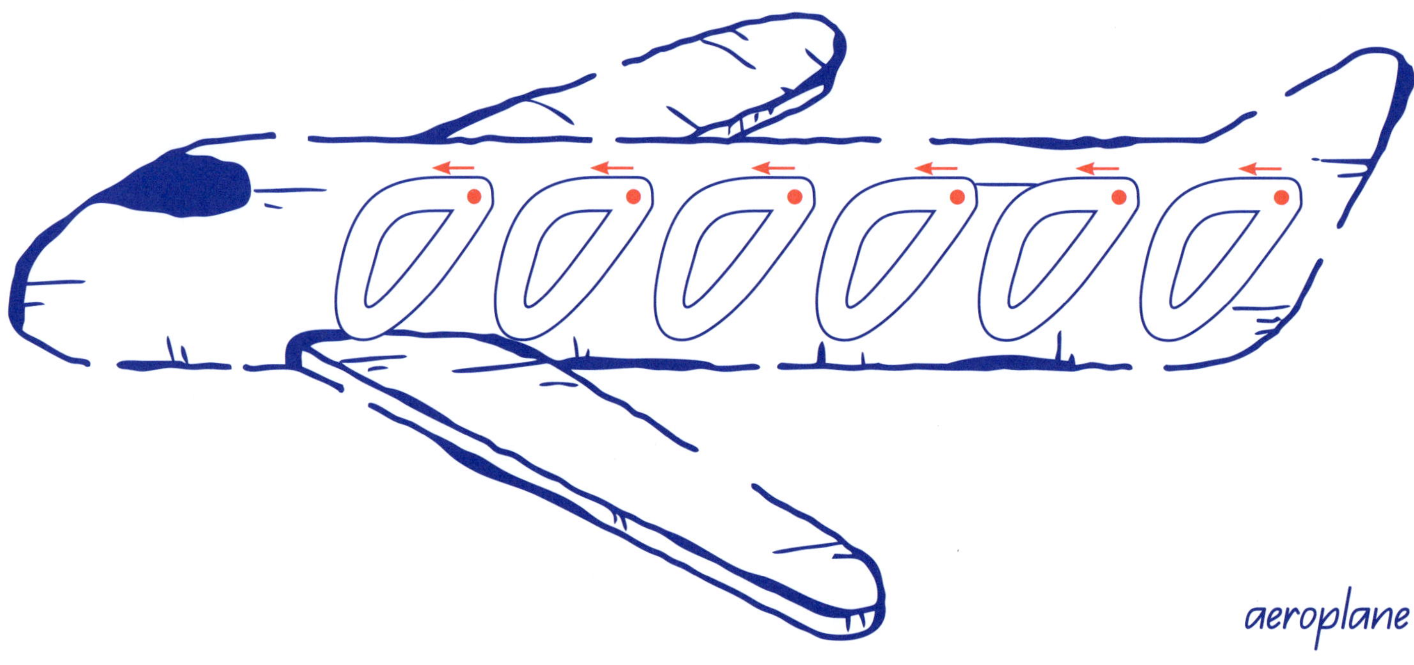

Track.

 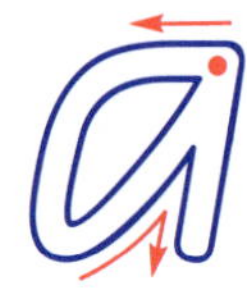   

Trace.

Anti-clockwise movement

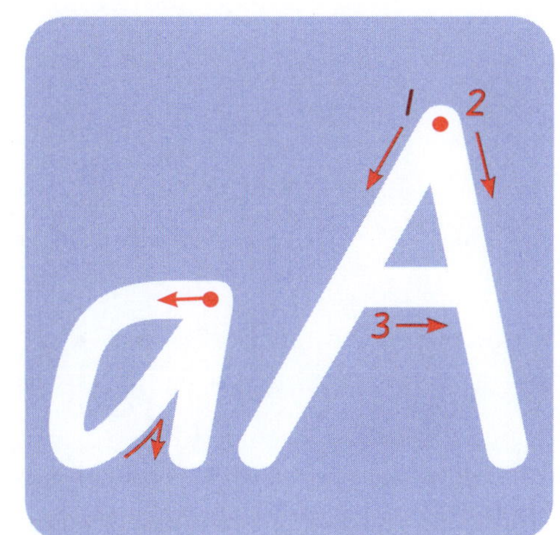

Track. Start at the red dot.

Trace.
Start at the red dot.

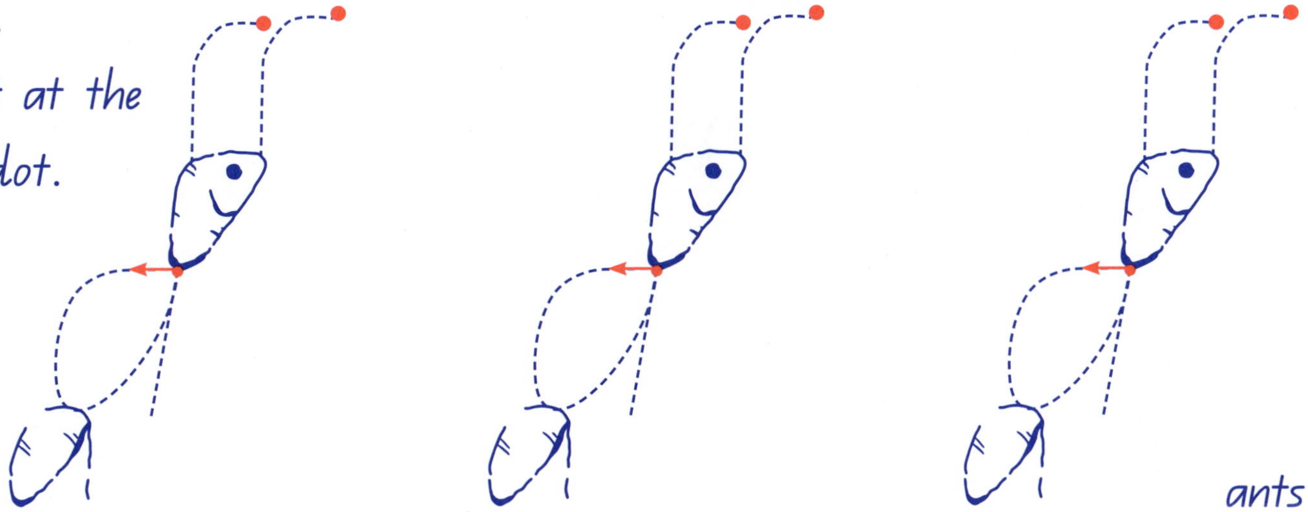

ants

Trace.

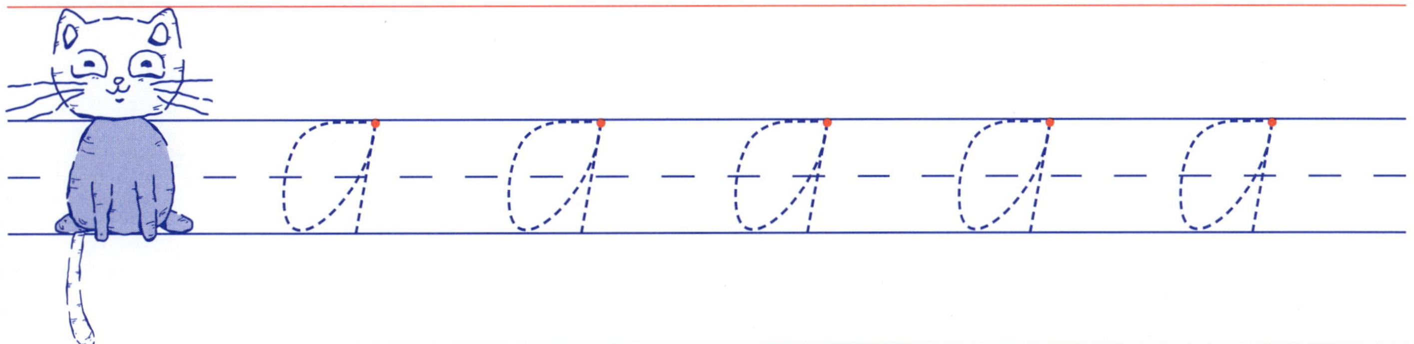

c

Track. Start at the red dot.

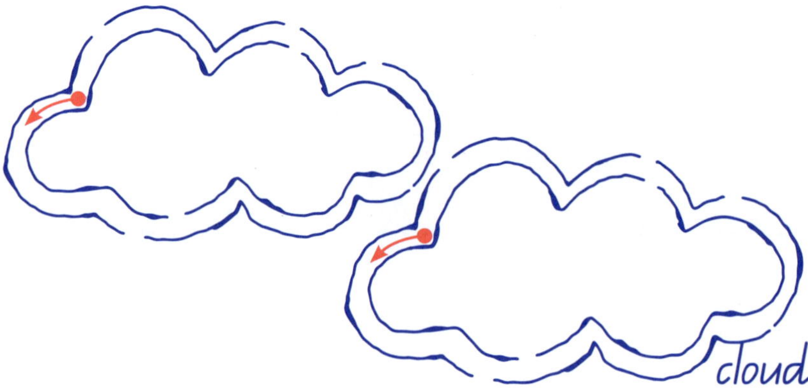

clouds

Trace. Start at the red dot.

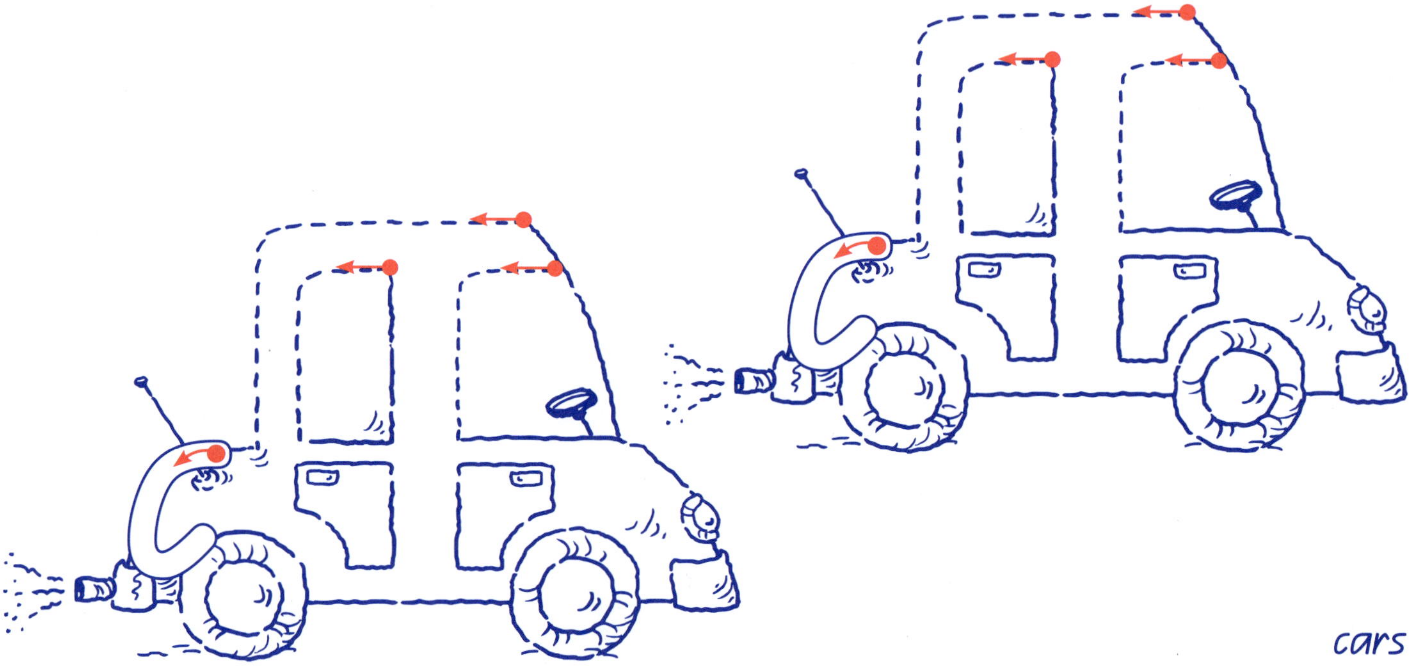

cars

Track.

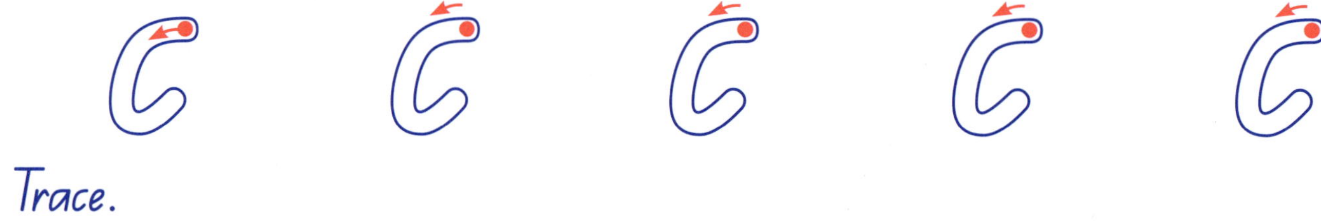

Trace.

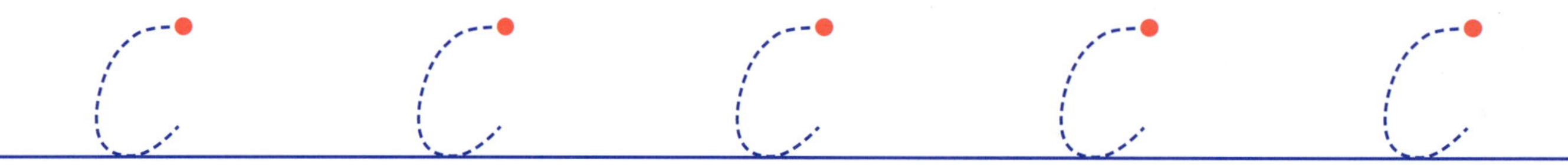

Anti-clockwise movement

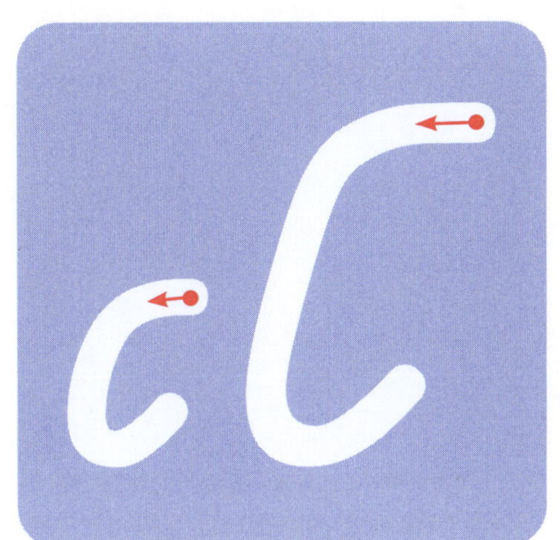

Track. Start at the red dot.

cups

cats

Trace.

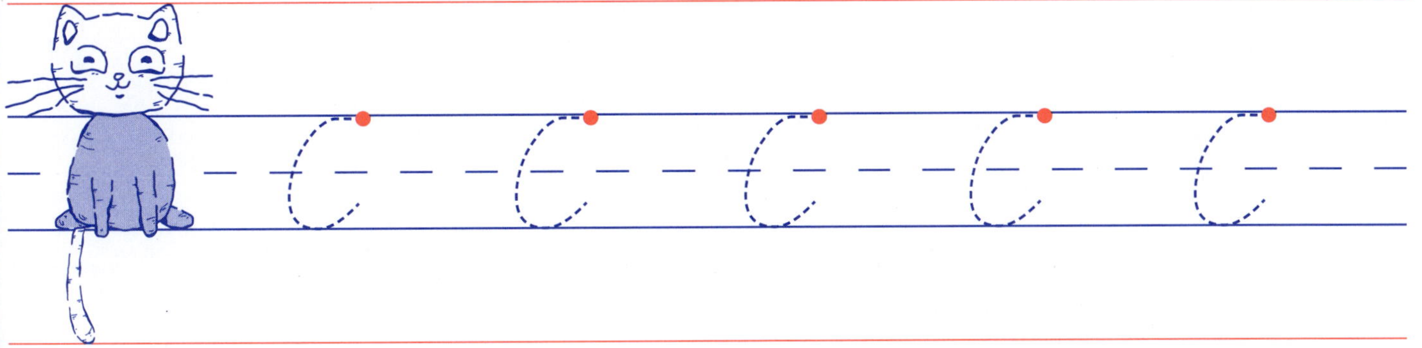

Trace. Start at the red dot.

octopuses

Track. Start at the red dot.

owls

Track.

Trace.

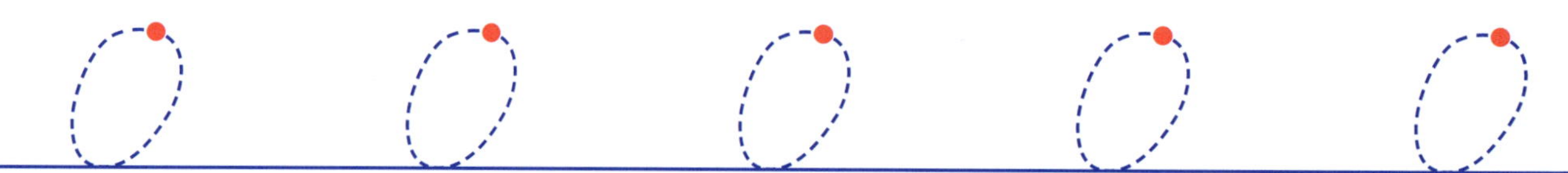

Anti-clockwise movement

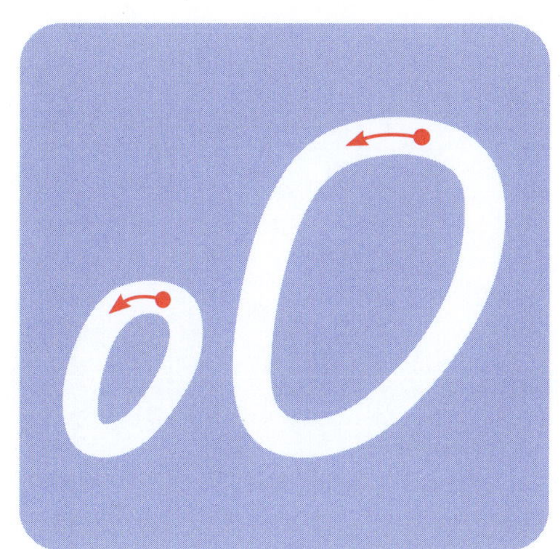

Trace. Start at the red dot.

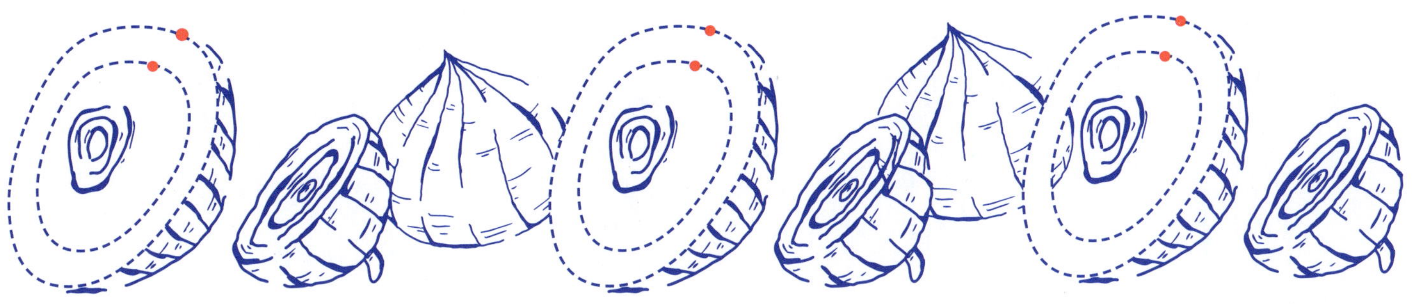

onions

Trace.

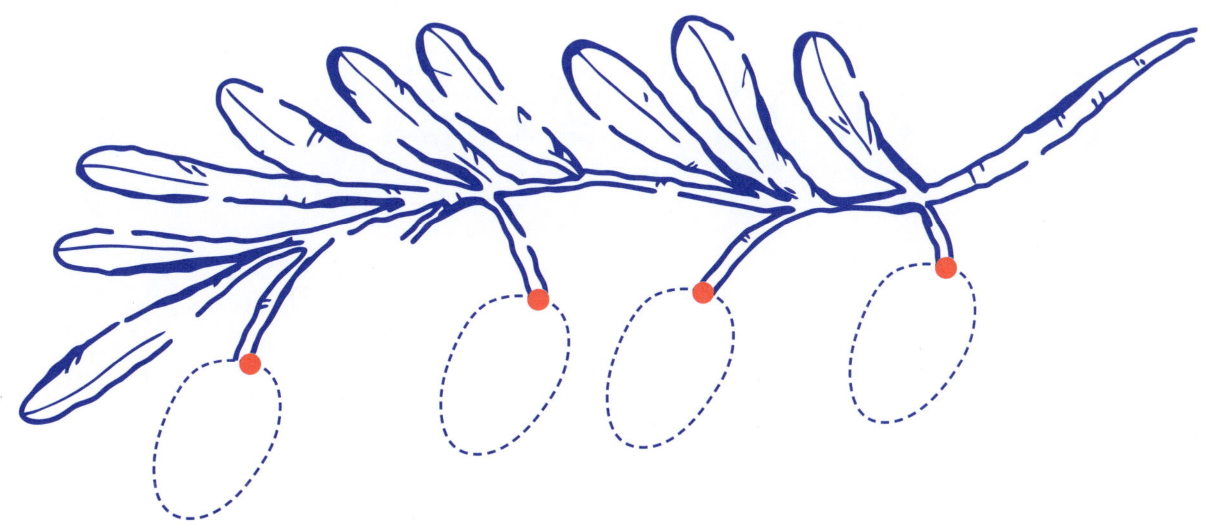

olives

Trace.

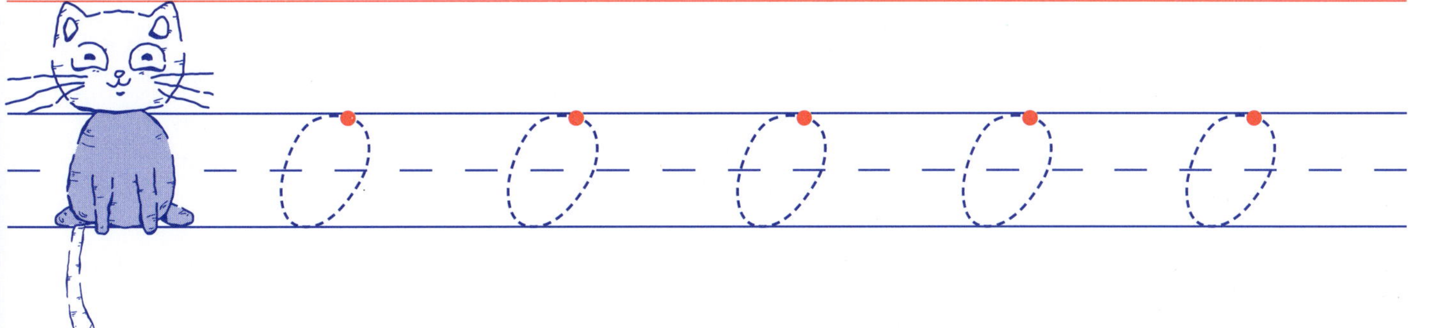

Trace. Start at the red dot.

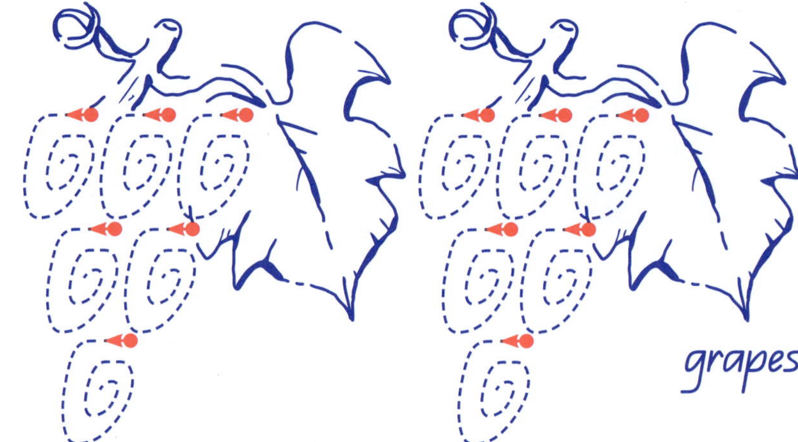

grapes

Track. Start at the red dot.

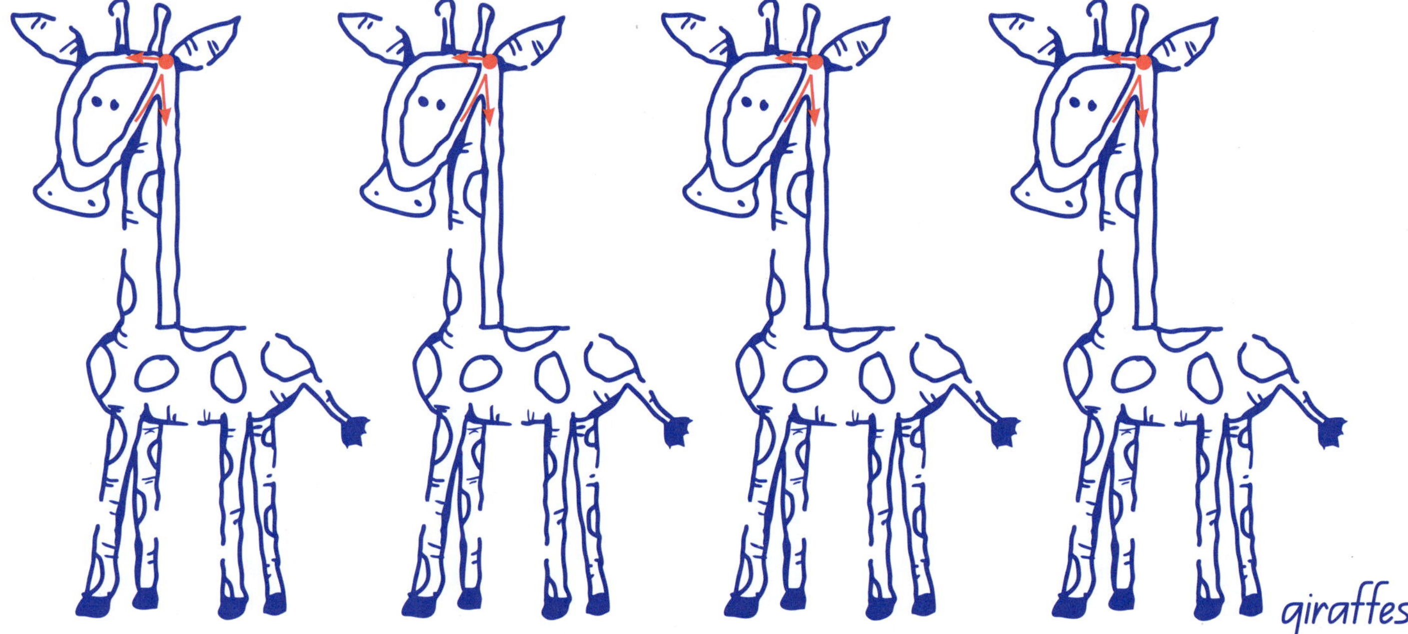

giraffes

Track.

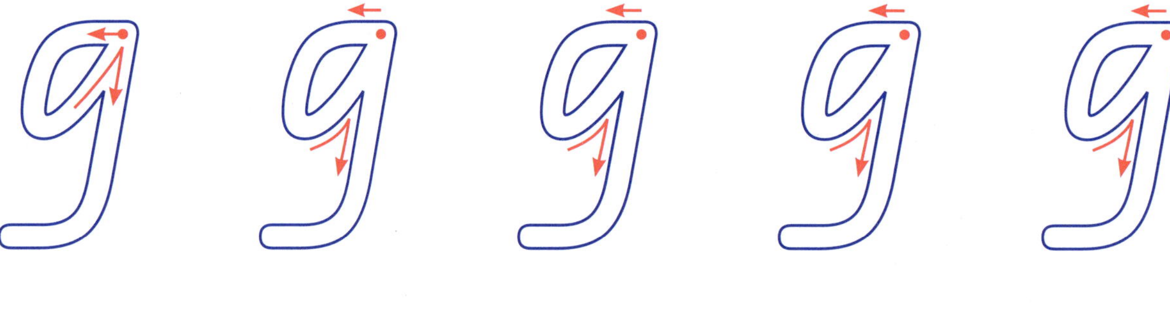

Trace.

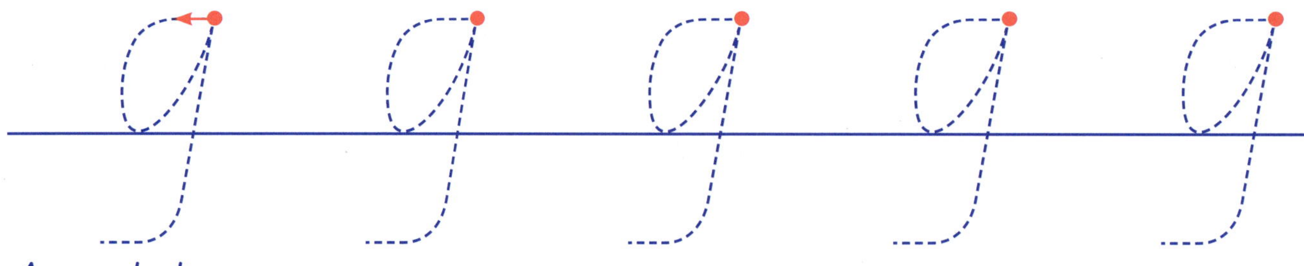

Anti-clockwise movement

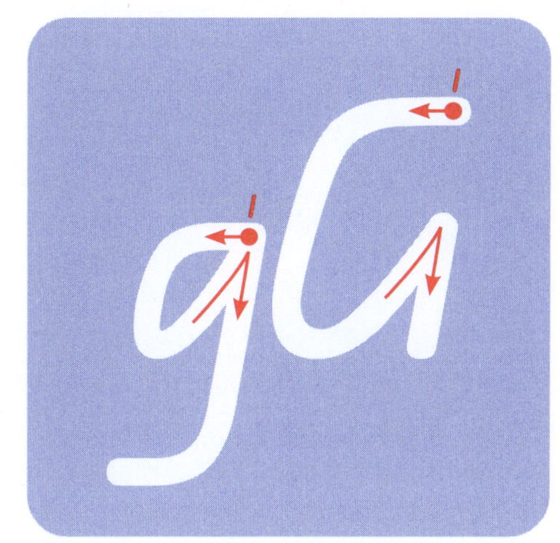

Track. Start at the red dot.

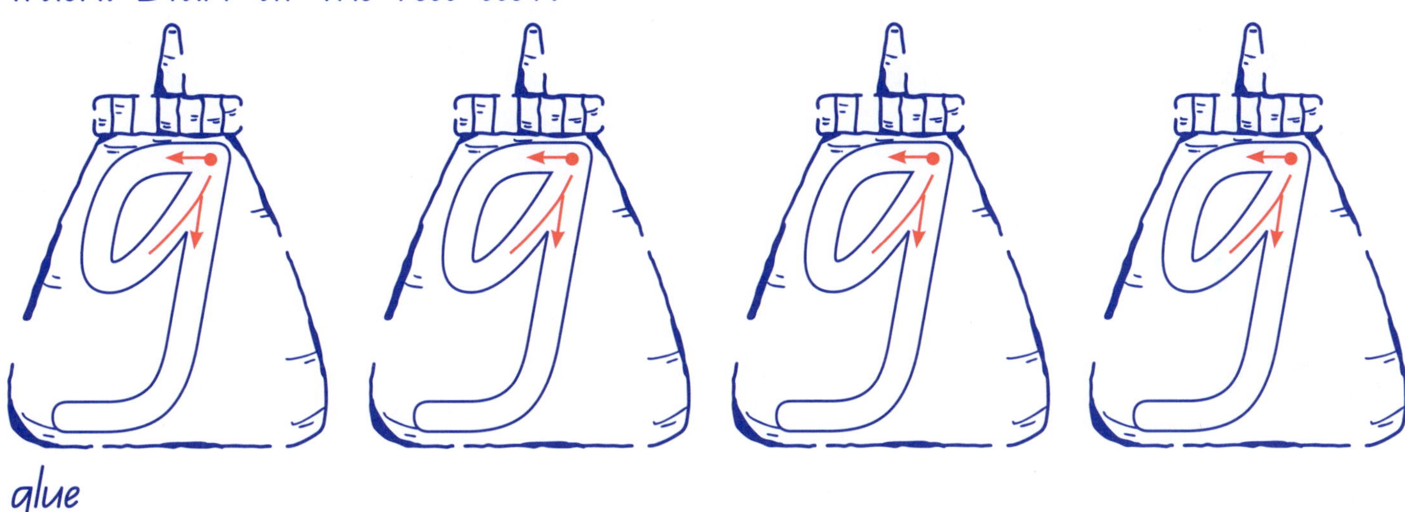

glue

girls

Trace.

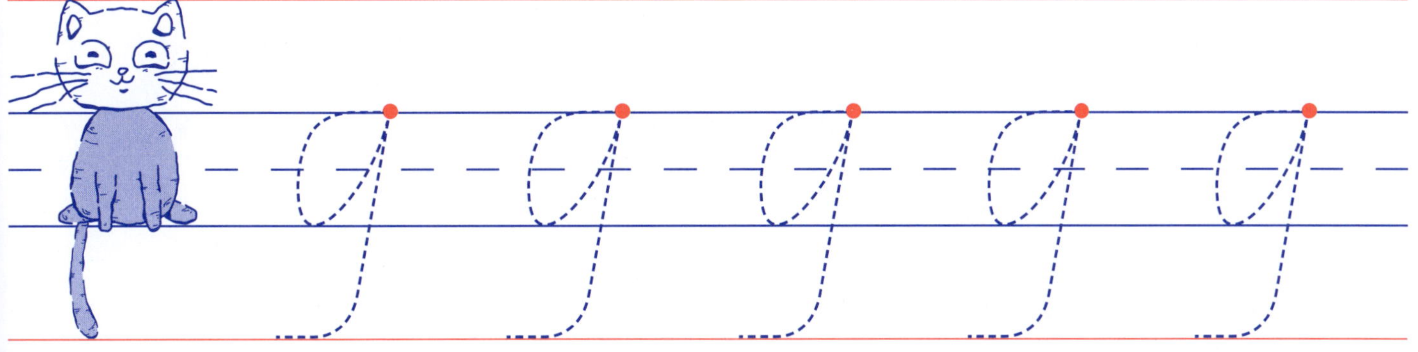

Track. Start at the red dot.

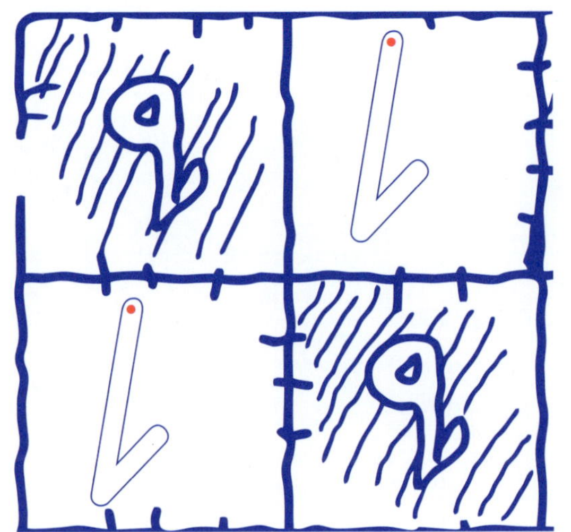

quilt

Trace. Start at the red dot.

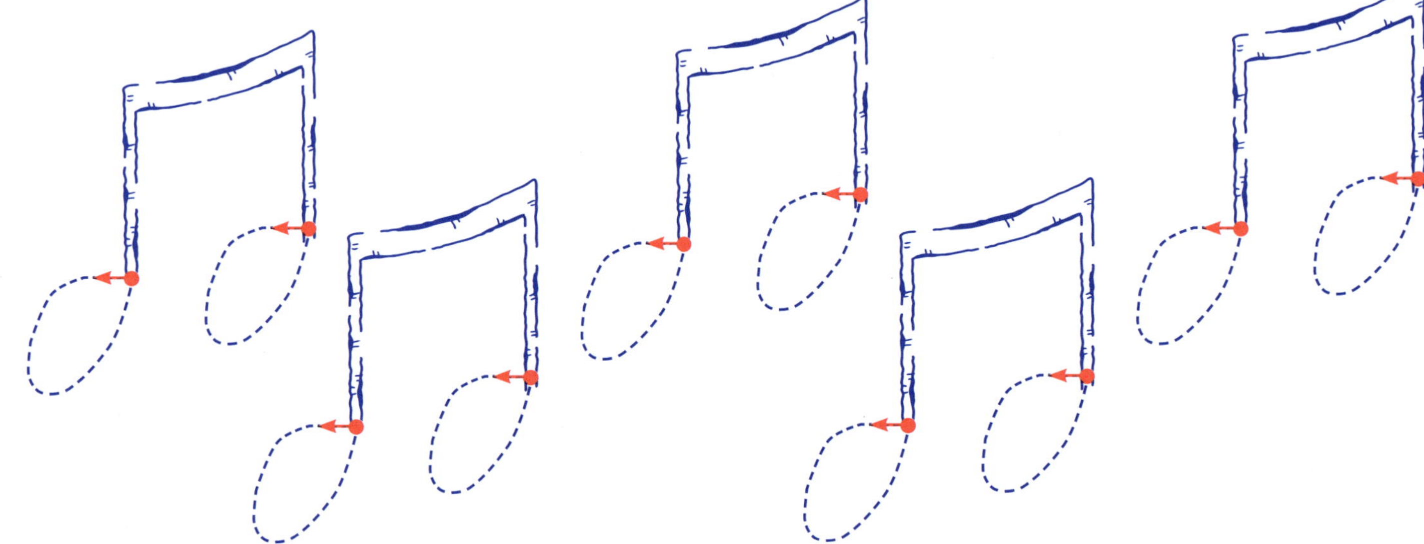

quavers

Track.

Trace.

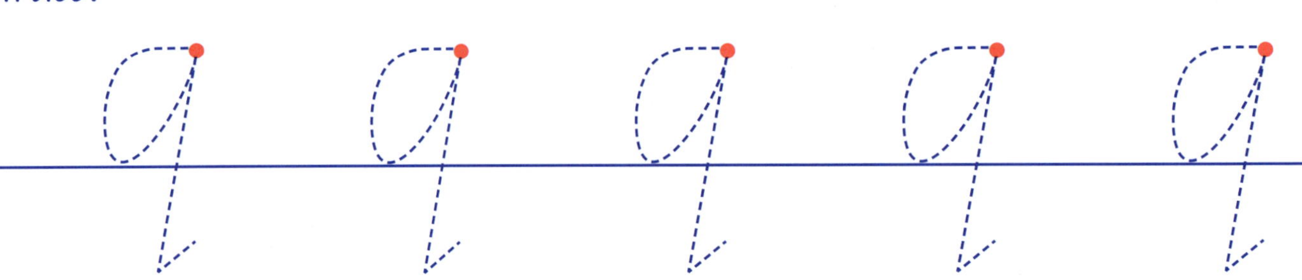

Anti-clockwise movement

Track. Start at the red dot.

Queens

Trace.

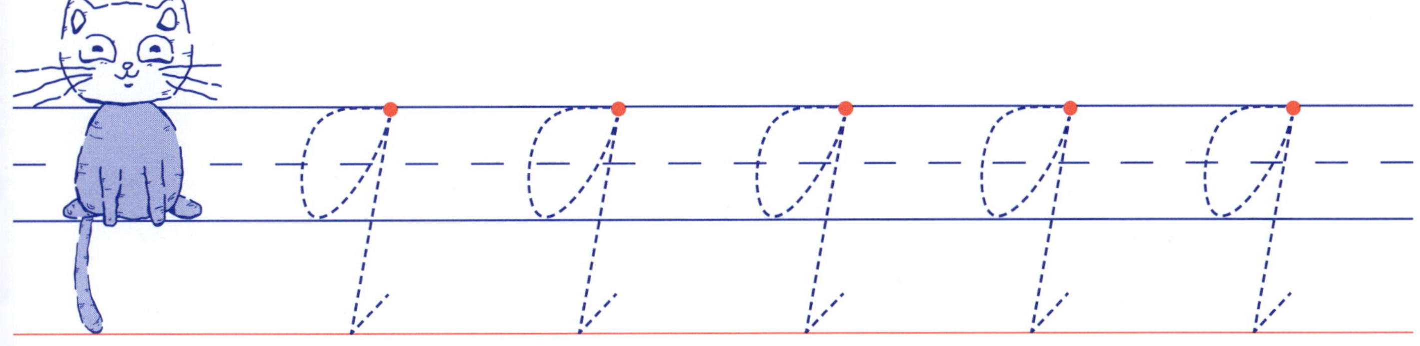

Trace. Start at the red dot.

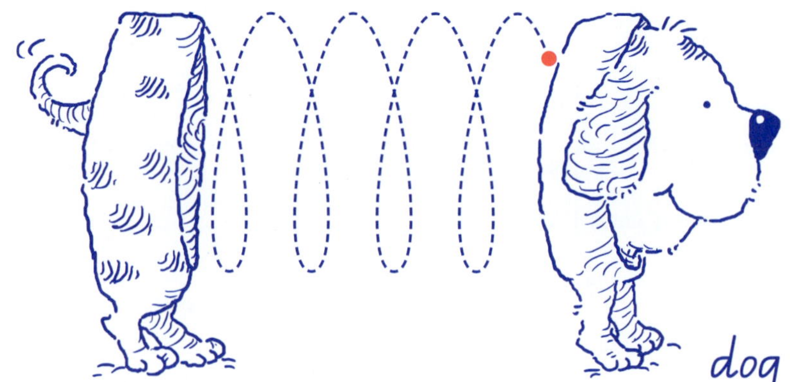

Track.

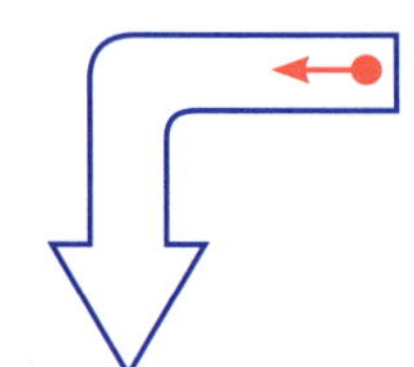
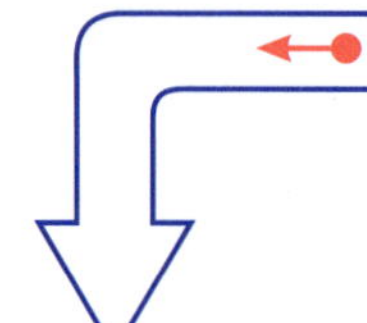
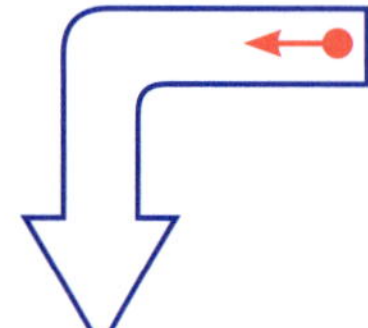
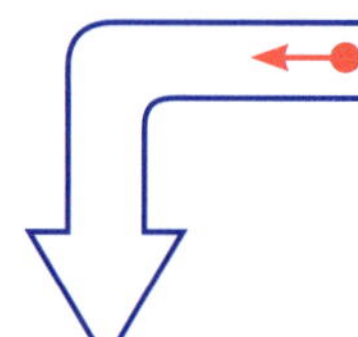
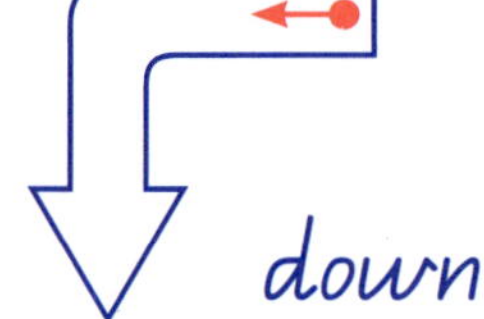

Trace.

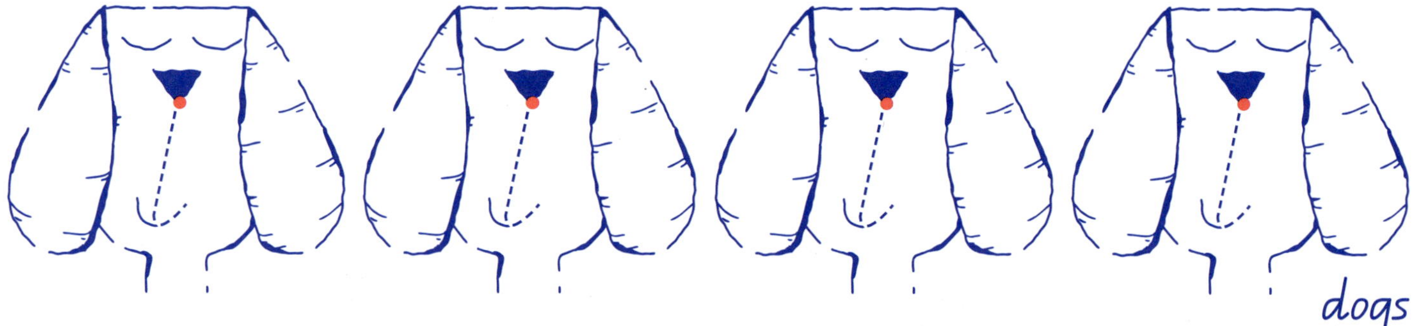

Track.

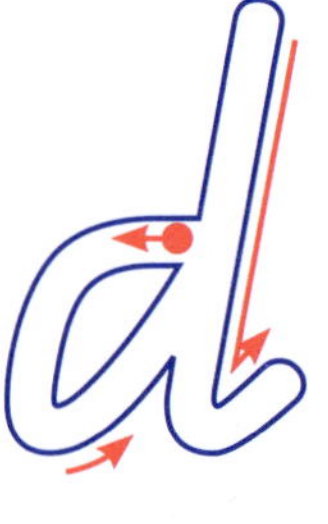

Trace.

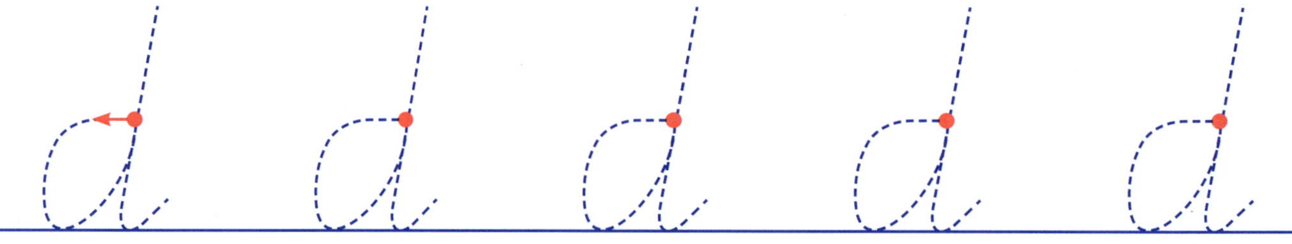

Anti-clockwise movement

a head and
body letter

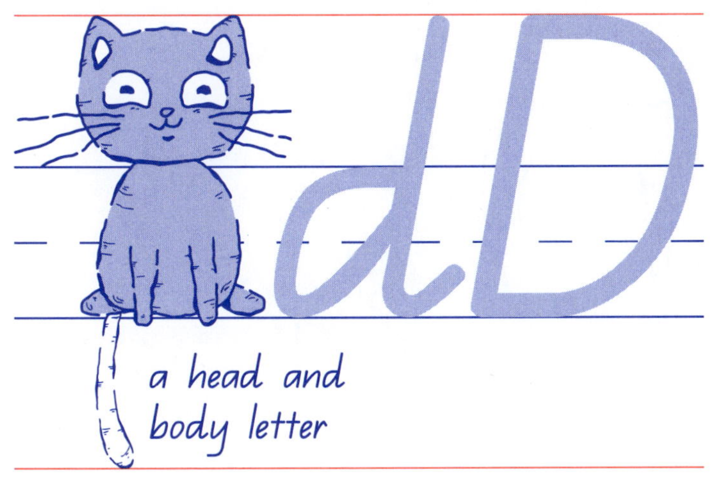

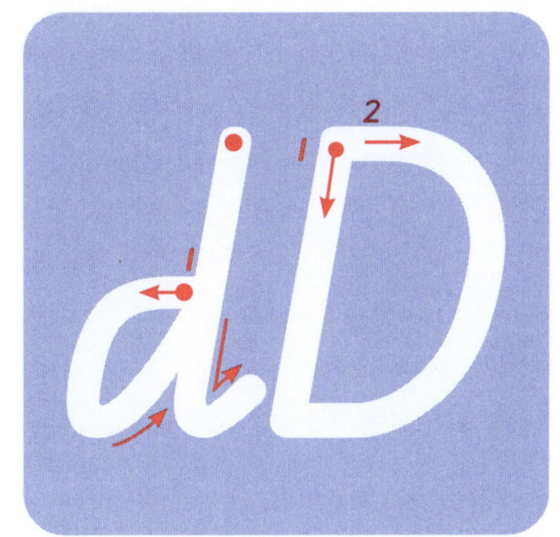

Trace. Start at the red dot.

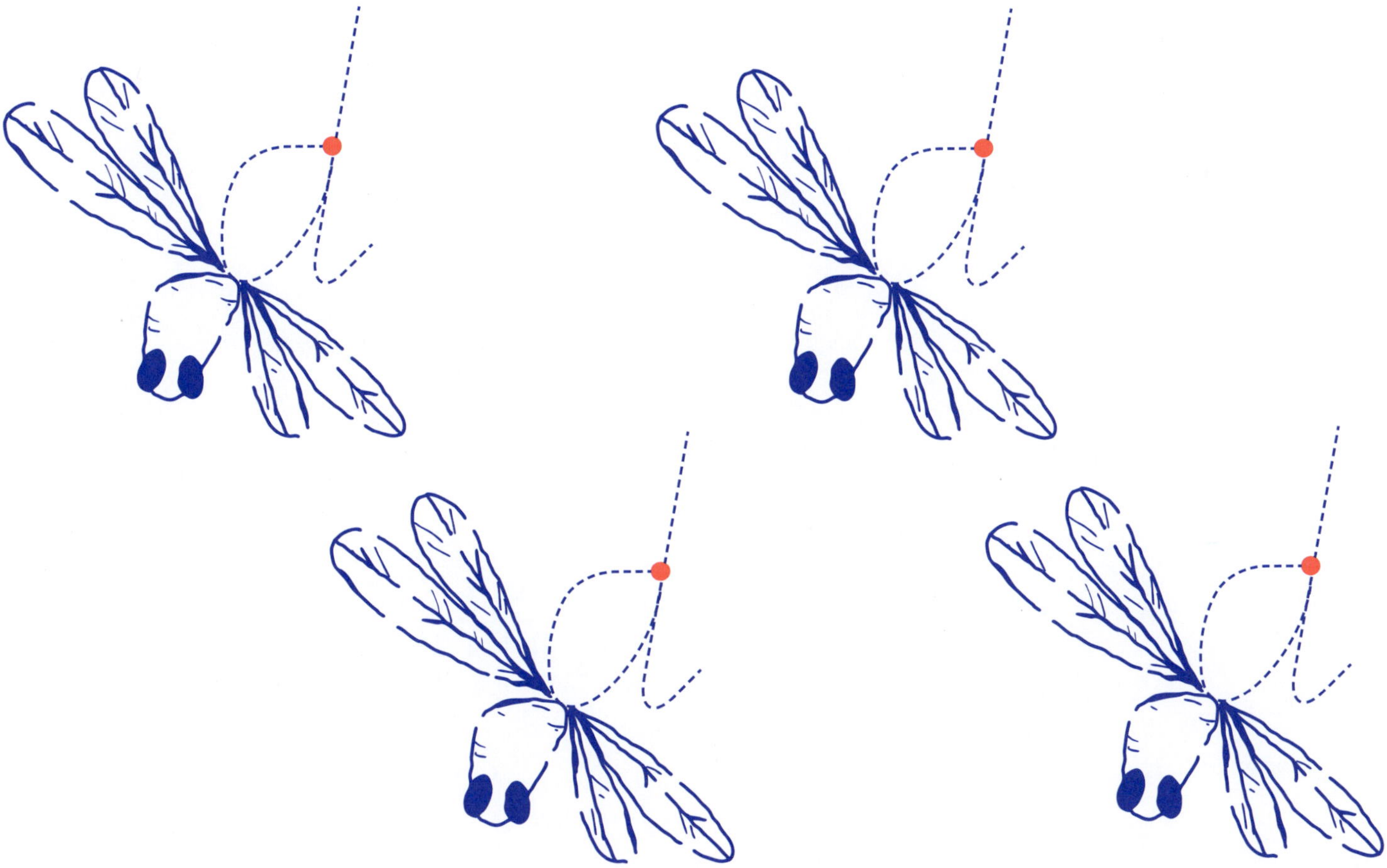

dragonflies

Trace.

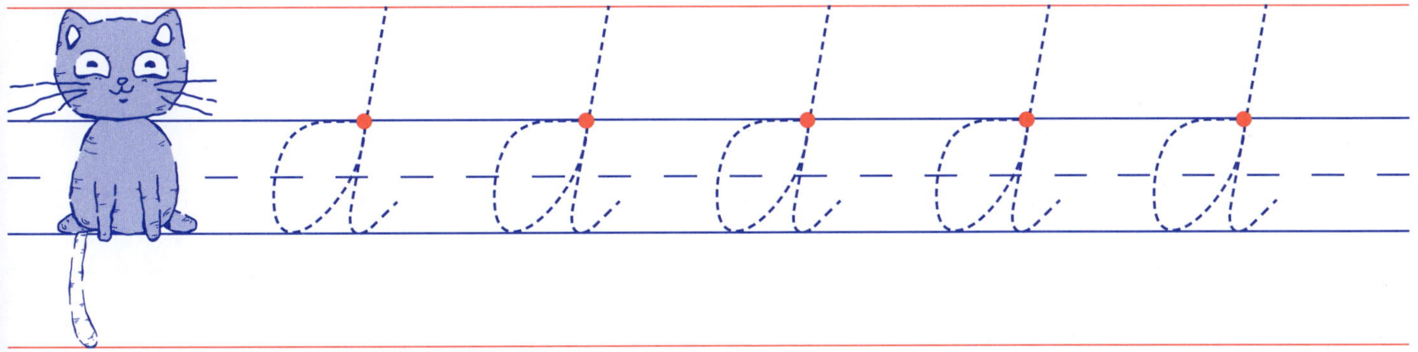

Track. Start at the red dot.

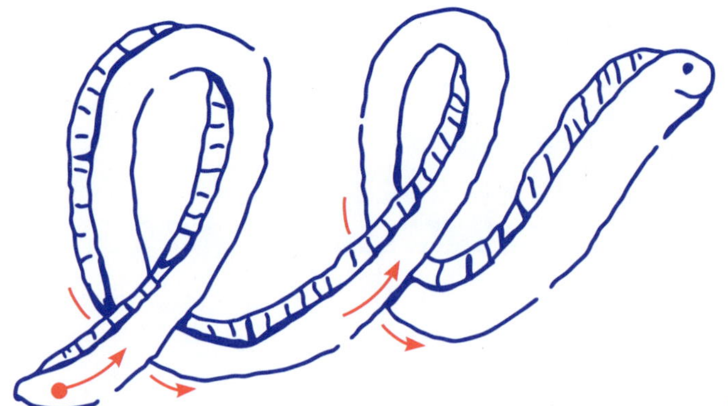

eel

Trace. Start at the red dot.

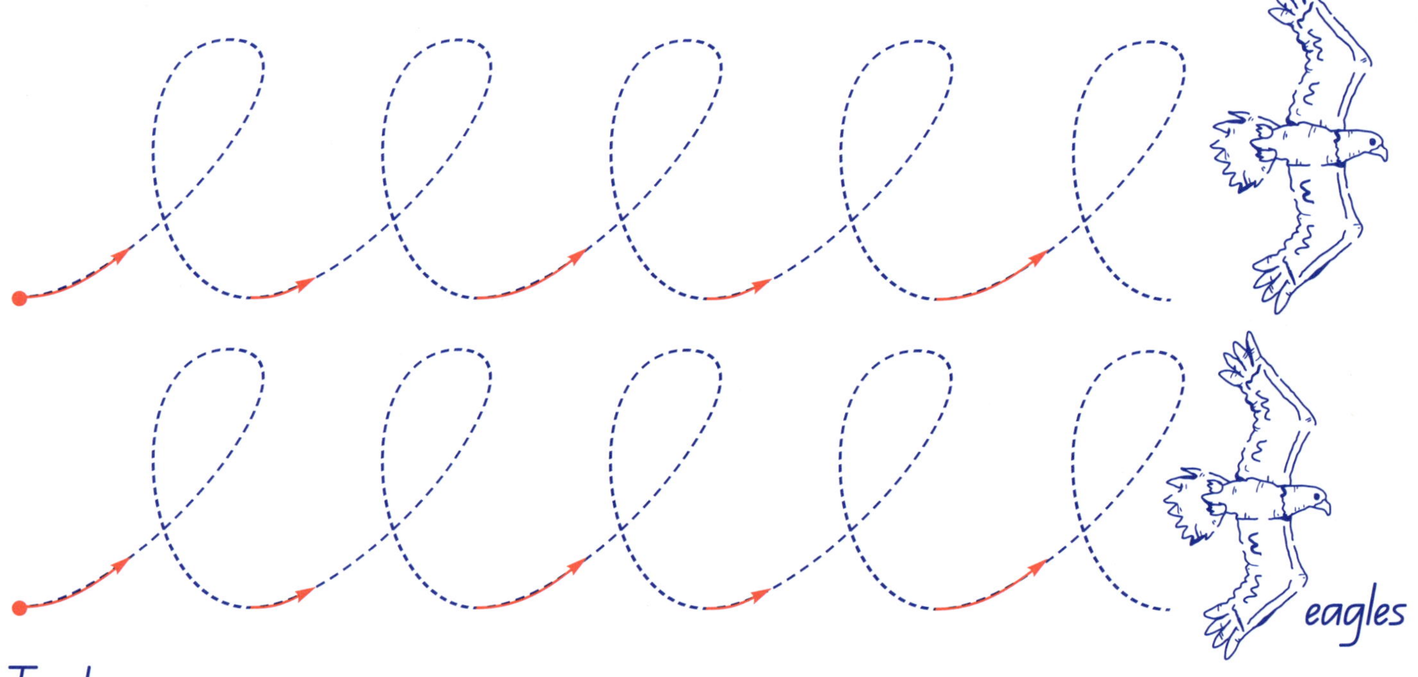

Track.

Trace.

Anti-clockwise movement

Trace. Start at the red dot.

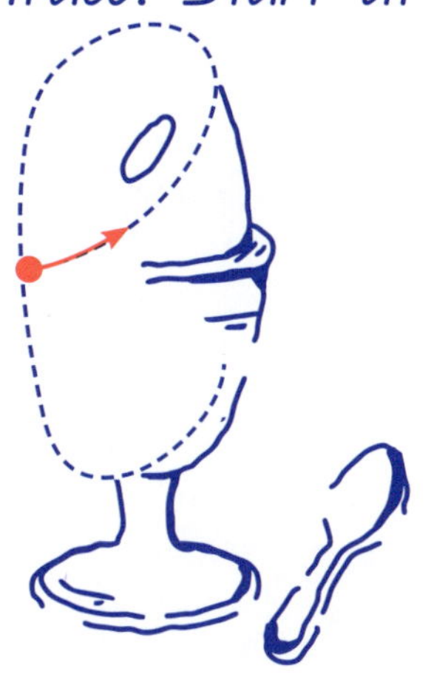

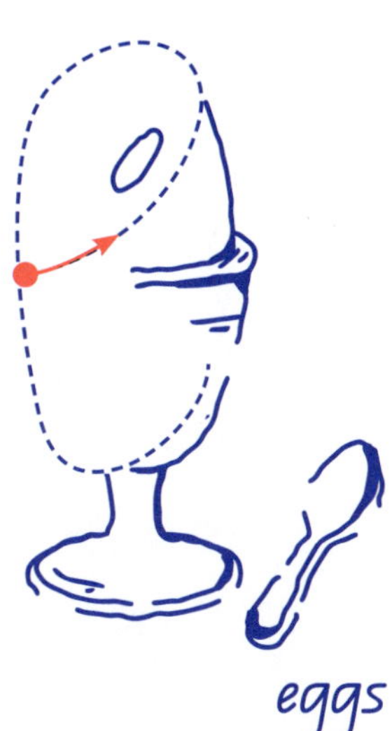

eggs

Track.

elephants

Trace.

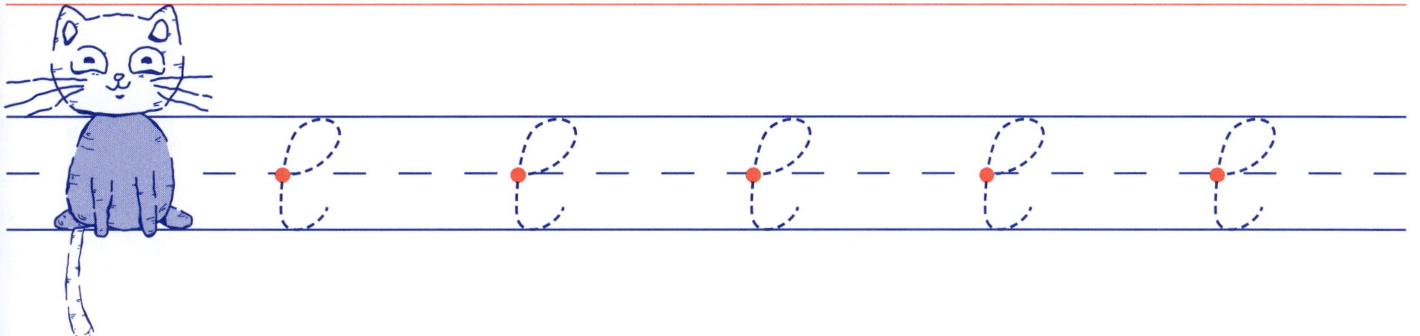

Track. Start at the red dot.

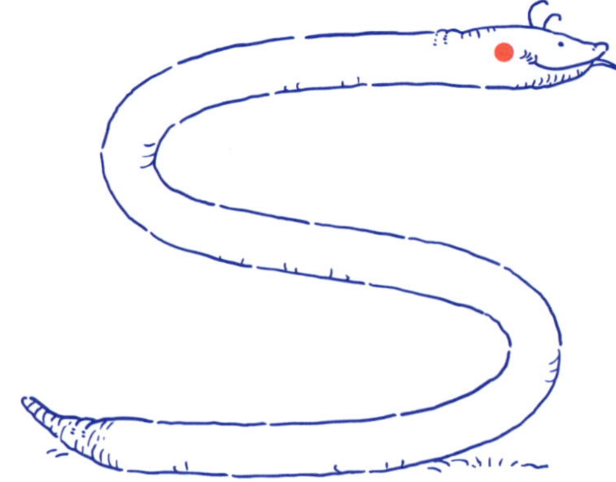

snake

Track. Start at the red dot.

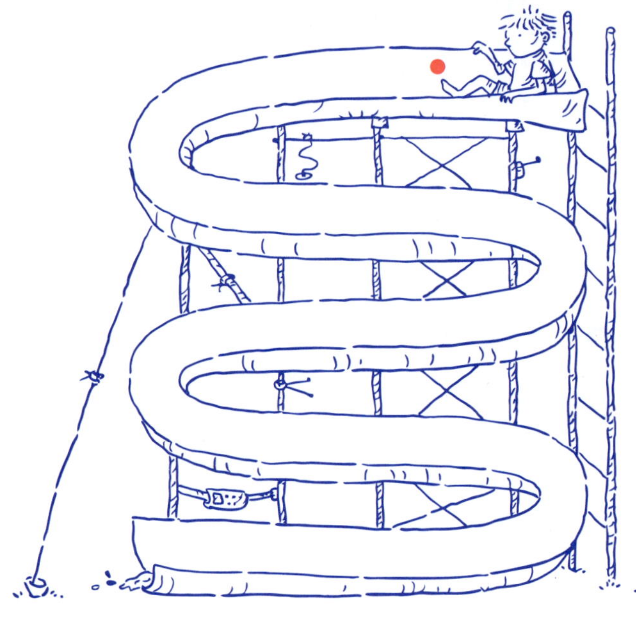

slippery slide

Track.

Trace.

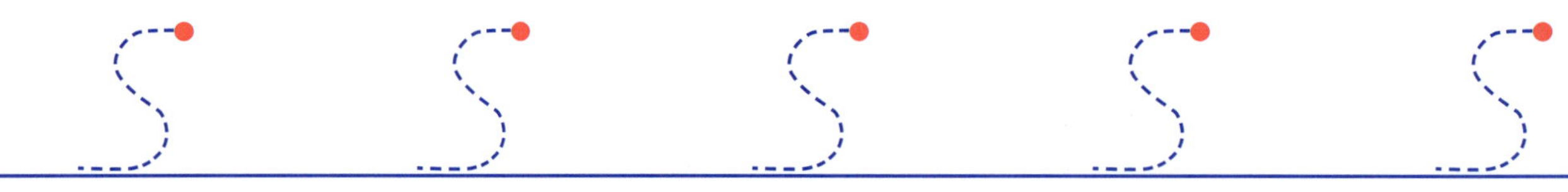

Anti-clockwise and clockwise movement

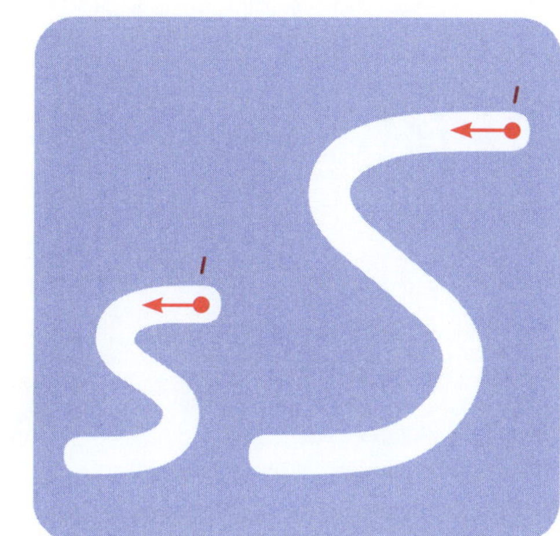

Trace. Start at the red dot.

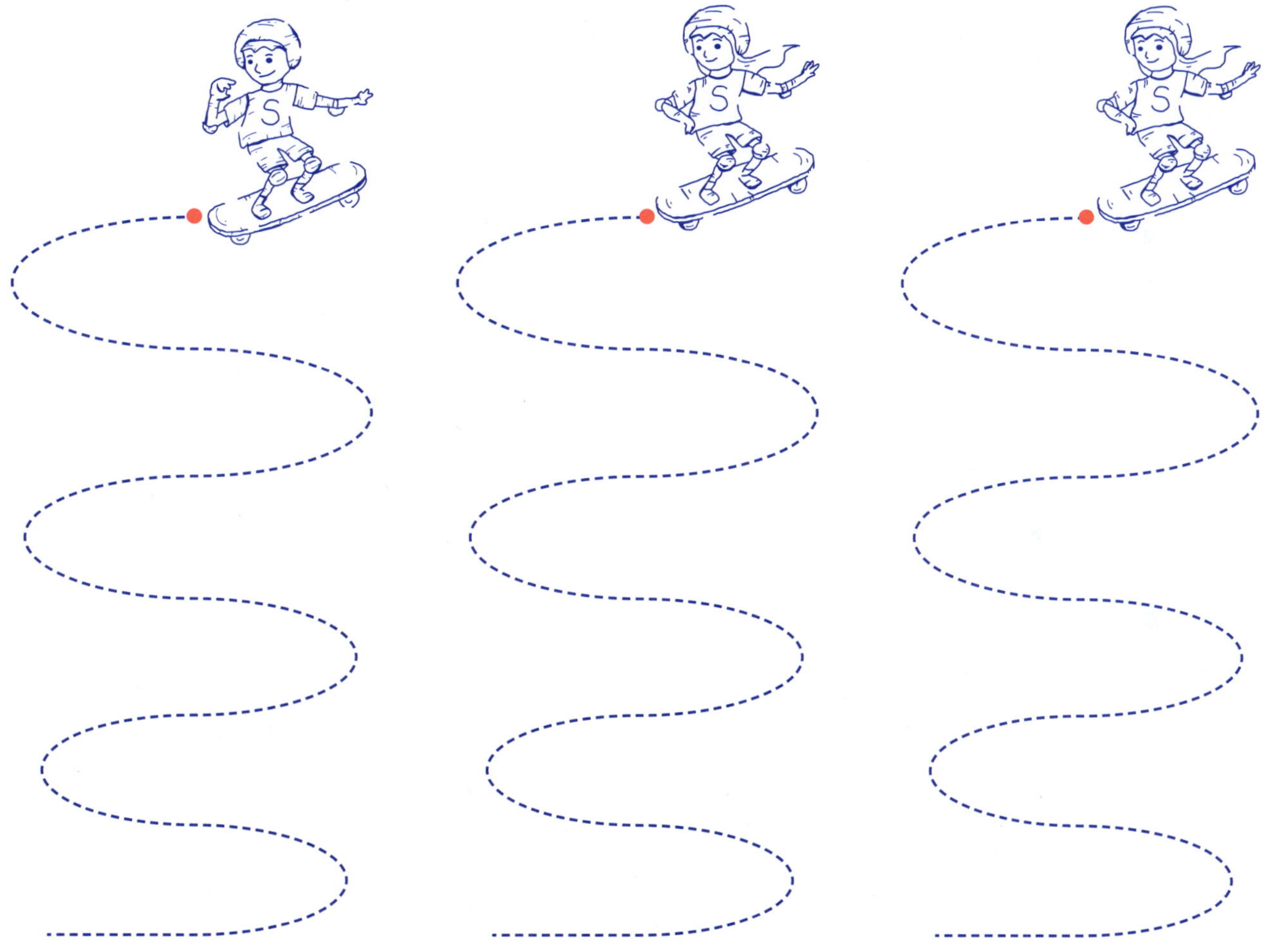

skate boarding

Trace.

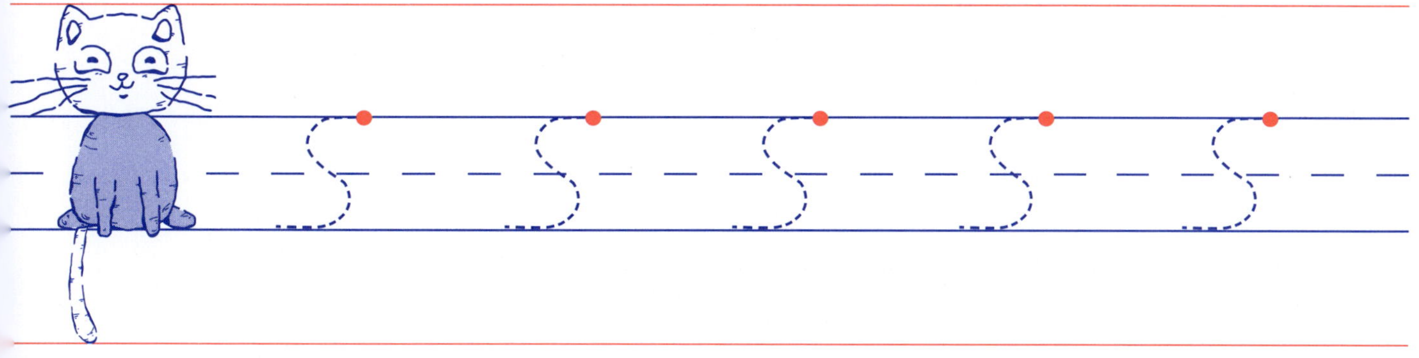

one

1

two

2

three

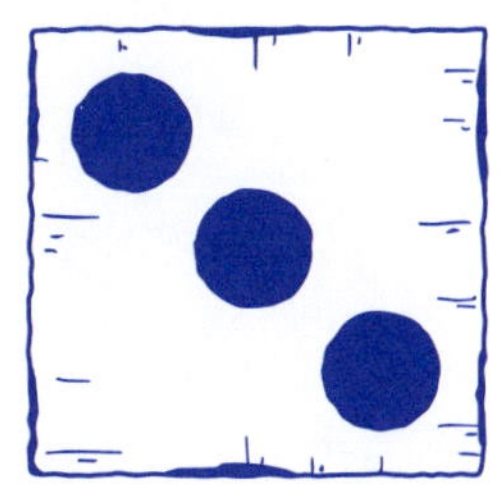

3

3 3 3 3 3

four

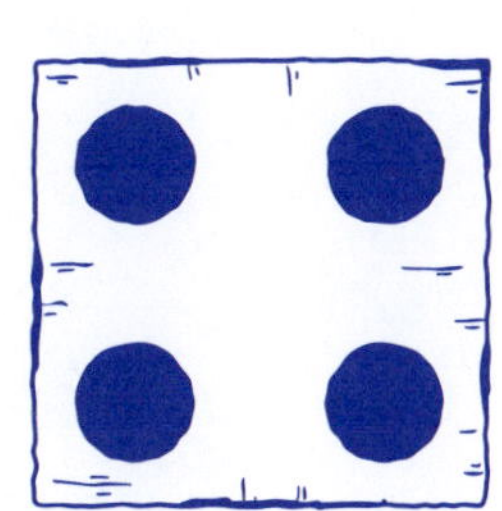

4

1

2

4 4 4 4 4

five

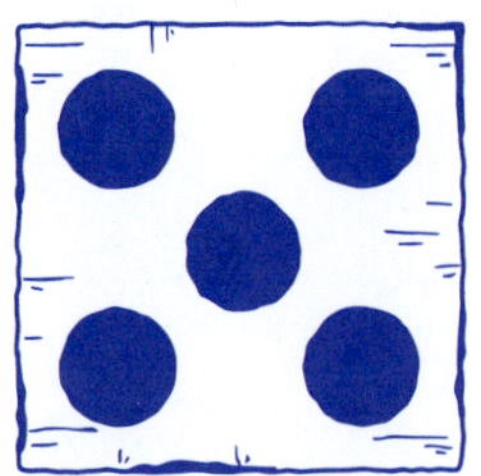

5

5 5 5 5 5

six

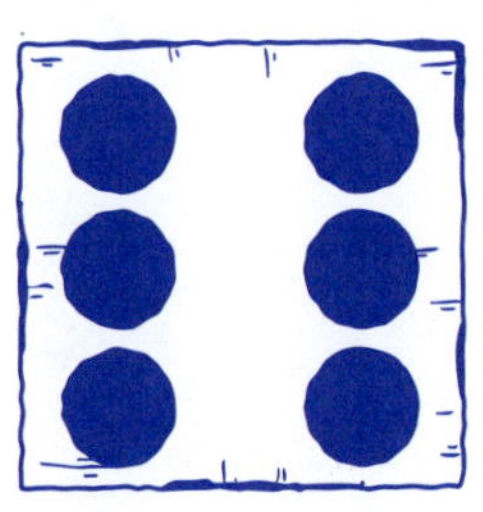

6

6 6 6 6 6

seven

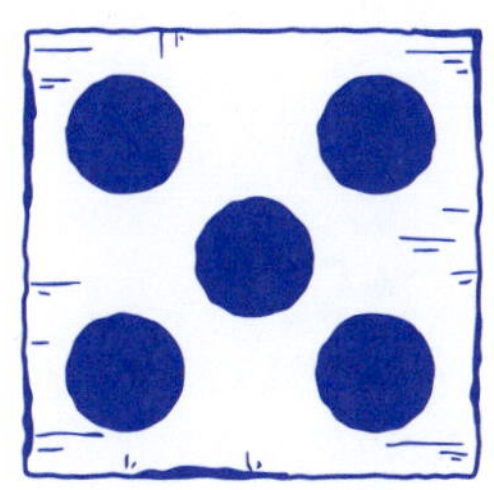
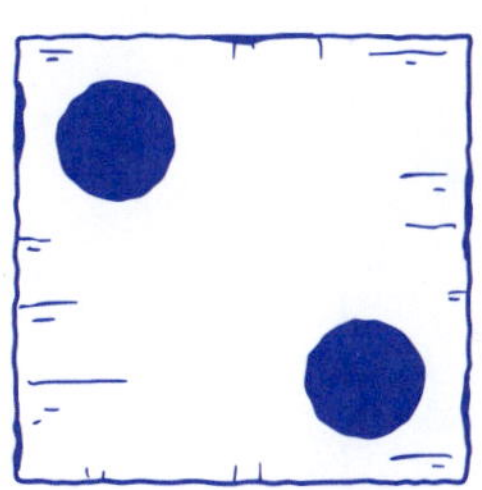

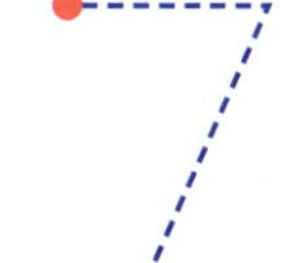
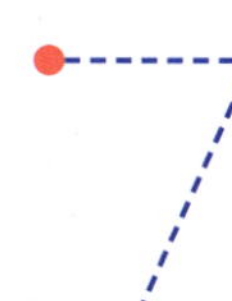
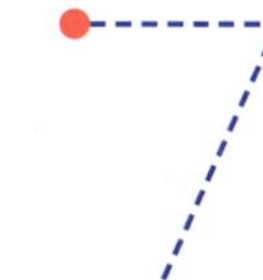

eight

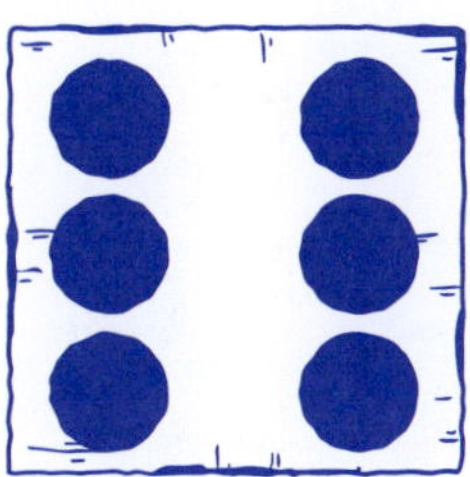
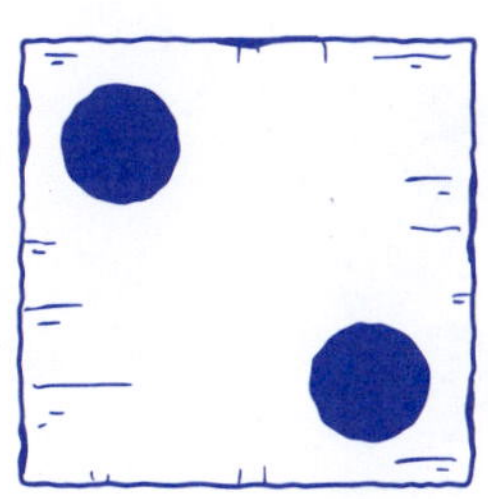

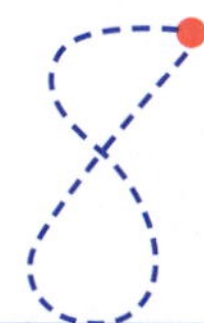

nine

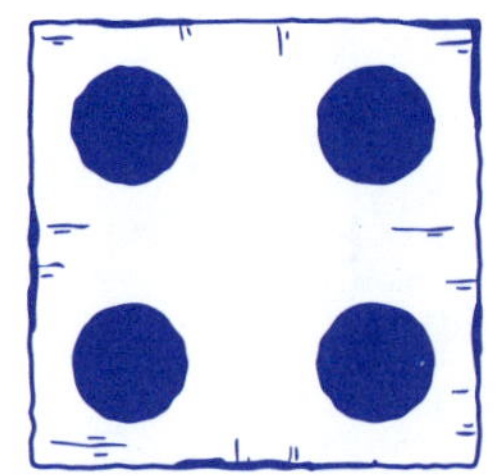

ten

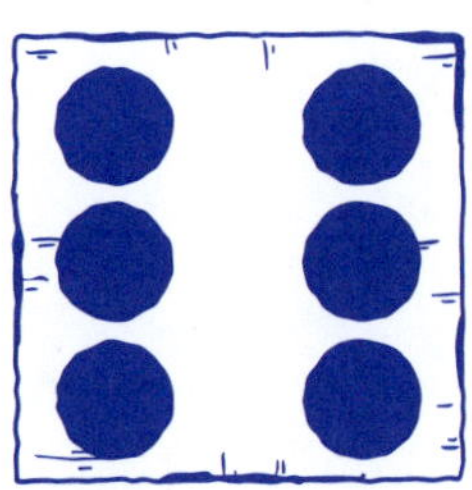
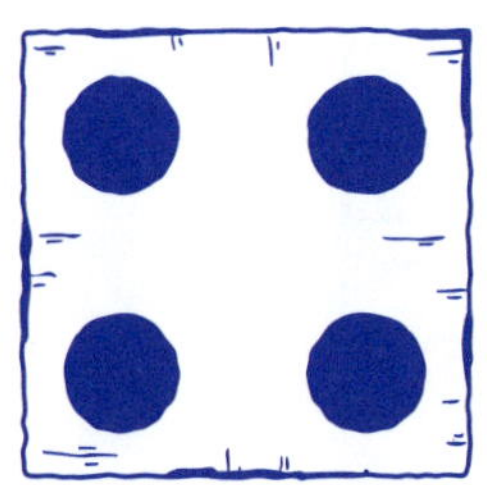

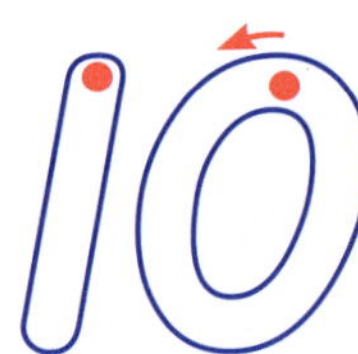
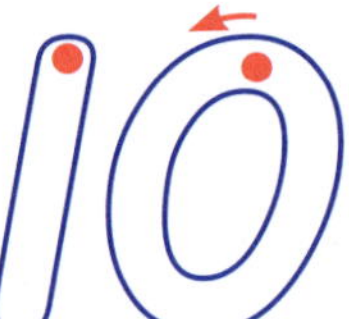

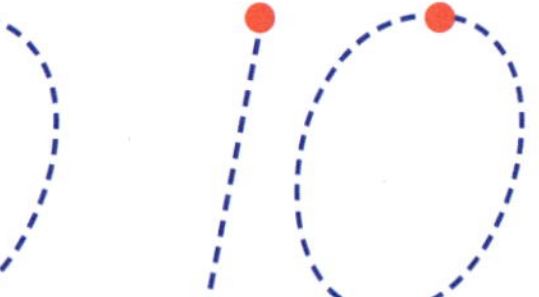
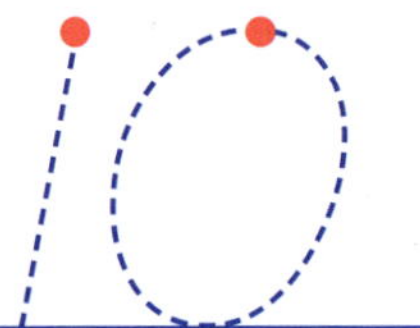
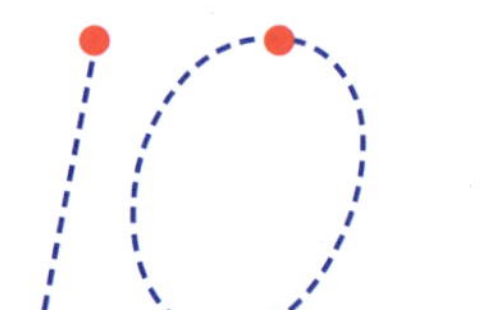
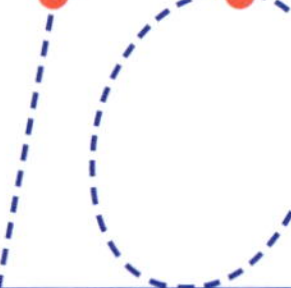

Well done ______________________.

Your writing is improving.

____

Teacher

____

Date

Congratulations ______________________.

Your writing is wonderful.

____

Teacher

____

Date